Johannes Weichart

Artificial Fingertip with
Embedded High Resolution
Tactile Sensing

Johannes Weichart

Artificial Fingertip with Embedded High Resolution Tactile Sensing

Hartung-Gorre Verlag Konstanz

Reprint of Diss. ETH No. 29376

Scientific Reports on Micro and Nanosystems　　　　**Volume 36**

edited by Prof. Dr. Christofer Hierold
ETH Zürich
Micro and Nanosystems

Cover images:
Front:.
- **Left: Artificial fingertip with integrated sensing array;**
- **Right: Electron microscope image of a tactile sensor;**

Back:
- **Left: Released sensing array on a human finger;**
- **Right: Overview of structural layers in a taxel;**

Bibliographic information published by Die Deutsche Nationalbibliothek

Die Deutsche Nationalbibliothek lists this publication in the Deutsche
Nationalbibliografie; detailed bibliographic data is available
in the internet at http://dnb.dnb.de.

First edition 2023

HARTUNG-GORRE VERLAG, KONSTANZ
http://www.hartung-gorre.de

ISSN 2566-7769

ISBN 978-3-86628-802-7

There is a theory which states that if ever anyone discovers exactly what the Universe is for and why it is here, it will instantly disappear and be replaced by something even more bizarre and inexplicable. There is another theory which states that this has already happened. – It is a mistake to think you can solve any major problems just with potatoes.

The Hitchhiker's Guide to the Galaxy, Douglas Adams

Diss. ETH No. 29376

Artificial Fingertip with Embedded High Resolution Tactile Sensing

A dissertation submitted to
ETH ZURICH
to attain the degree of
Doctor of Sciences
(Dr. sc. ETH Zurich)

presented by
Johannes Weichart
MSc. in Mechanical Engineering, ETH Zurich

born January 12th, 1991
citizen of Liechtenstein

accepted on the recommendation of

Prof. Dr. Christofer Hierold, examiner
Prof. Dr. Herbert Shea, co-examiner
Prof. Dr. Clementine Boutry, co-examiner

2023

Abstract

The replication of the human sense of touch in robots or prostheses would greatly enhance their ability to interact with the environment. This thesis investigates the possibility to rebuild a human fingertip with its mechanical sensing capabilities. A soft, human-sized artificial fingertip was developed, equipped with an array of 144 tactile sensors (taxels). These 0.5 mm diameter taxels can detect touch, vibrations, and shear, enabling the artificial finger to distinguish between different external stimuli.

This thesis describes the design of the taxels, the fabrication as well as the characterization. The taxels can sense pressures with a sensitivity of 2.6 kPa^{-1} and were tested in a temperature range of 20 - 80°C as well as over 10'000 cycles. The sensing characteristics are determined by the thickness of a spray-coated silicone layer that encases the sensors, increasing their robustness to external influences. The static and dynamic sensing capabilities of the encapsulated taxels were evaluated. The sensitivity can be modified according to the needs of an application. Skin thicknesses between 0 - 660µm allowed sensitivities of 0.86 - 0.035 kPa^{-1}. A similar trend was observed for dynamic sensing capabilities.

The softness of a human finger was measured to create an artificial finger of similar conformity. Simulation results supported the transfer of taxel characteristics from on-chip to the soft fingertip. Miniaturized readout electronics allowed to read the full finger at 220 Hz, enabling the observation of touch and slipping events on the artificial finger and the estimation of the contact force. Slipping events can be detected as vibrations registered by individual sensors, while the contact force can be estimated by averaging sensor array readouts. The robustness of the fingers was tested by applying 15 N for >2000 times, which resulted in only minor degradation in stiffened membranes. Neural networks were tested to extract simple features like object recognition or the evaluation of contact force and location. Good classification scores of ∼90% could be achieved on an early version of the artificial finger.

Zusammenfassung

Die Nachbildung des menschlichen Tastsinns kann Robotern oder Prothesen helfen, besser mit der Umwelt zu interagieren. Diese Arbeit untersucht die Möglichkeit, eine menschliche Fingerspitze mit ihrem mechanischen Tastsinn nachzubauen. Die entwickelte künstliche Fingerspitze mit der Weichheit und Grösse eines menschlichen Fingers ist mit 144 taktilen Sensoren (Taxels) ausgestattet. Diese 0.5 mm grossen Taxels können Berührungen, Vibrationen und Scherkräfte erkennen, sodass der künstliche Finger zwischen verschiedenen externen Reizen unterscheiden kann.

Die These beschreibt das Design der Taxel, die Herstellung sowie die Charakterisierung. Die Taxels können Drücke mit einer Empfindlichkeit von 2.6 kPa^{-1} messen und wurden in einem Temperaturbereich von 20 - 80°C sowie über 10'000 Zyklen getestet. Die Sensoreigenschaften werden durch die Dicke einer aufgesprühten Silikonschicht bestimmt, die die Sensoren umhüllt und ihre Robustheit gegenüber äusseren Einflüssen erhöht. Die statischen und dynamischen Eigenschaften der eingekapselten Taxel wurden gemessen. Die Empfindlichkeit kann entsprechend den Anforderungen verschiedener Anwendungen modifiziert werden, indem die Dicke der Schutzschicht variiert wird. Dicken zwischen 0 - 660 µm erlaubten Empfindlichkeiten von 0,86 - 0,035 kPa^{-1}. Ein ähnlicher Trend wurde für dynamische Messfähigkeiten beobachtet.

Die Thesis beschreibt die Entwicklung eines künstlichen Fingers mit ähnlicher Flexibilität wie die eines menschliches Fingers. Simulationen erlaubten die Übersetzung der auf dem Chip gemessenen Taxel-Eigenschaften auf die weiche Spitze des künstlichen Fingers. Eine miniaturisierte Elektronik mit einer Auslesefrequenz von 220 Hz ermöglichte die kontinuierliche Messung von Berührungs- und Rutschvorgängen sowie die Schätzung der Kontaktkraft. Rutschereignisse konnten als Vibrationen erkannt werden, die von einzelnen Sensoren erfasst wurden. Der Mittelwert aller Taxels erlaubt hingegen die Abschätzung der Kontaktkraft. Die Robustheit des Fingers wurde getestet, indem er über 2000 Mal mit einer Kraft von 15 N beansprucht wurde, was zu einer geringen Degradation in versteiften Membranen führte. Erste Tests mit neuronale Netzen erlaubten die Erkennung von Objekten oder die Extraktion der Kontaktkraft und des Kontaktpunkts. Mit einer frühen Version des künstlichen Fingers konnten gute Klassifikations-werte von etwa 90% erzielt werden.

Acknowledgements

This thesis was written over the course of roughly four years, of which two years fell into the Covid pandemic. Both professional and social support were at least equally crucial over those years. I hereby would like to express my gratitude to everyone who helped me in this time, even if I might have forgot to list you in those words.

My professional environment was largely shaped by the research group, the work with project students as well as collaborators. My gratitude goes to Prof. Christofer Hierold, who helped to shape my doctorate and give me the possibility to work on this fascinating topic. The exchange with the whole research group was valuable and I especially want to appreciate Dr. Cosmin Roman's time for conceptual discussions as well as Florin Püntener's motivation in continuing some of the work. 21 students were a great help for my thesis in 23 performed student theses, their names and contributions are found in the list of publications (the list was simply too long for those words). Their collaboration and work they put into their theses, but also their interest in the topic and the scientific and social exchange were very valuable to me. It gave me the sense of working in a young and highly dynamic team.

The interdisciplinarity of the presented work would hardly have been possible without the support from various lab responsibles and collaborators. I would like to thank the BRNC cleanroom team, and especially Ute Drechsler, for their great support over the years and allowing smooth lab work. Additionally, I would like to thank the FIRST-CLA cleanroom team for the same purpose. The design of readout electronics would not have been possible without the help of Dr. Thomas Burger and the implementation support by Thomas Kleier. Dr. Fergal Coulter's support in soft material questions and the setup of the spray coating process helped to swiftly get into this new topic. The collaboration with the Robotics Systems Lab helped to understand the exciting potential of neural networks. For this I would like to thank Mayank Mittal, Dr. Firas Farraj and Prof. Marco Hutter. I also would like to thank my examiners (and co-advisor) Prof. Herbert Shea and Prof. Clementine Boutry for the scientific exchange and ideas, the work they put into this thesis and their interest.

My social environment was very important during those years, and naming everyone would be difficult. Two people from the research group grew into very good friends. With Ian (Jan Pillemann) I not only spent hours in the lab, but also many hours at home, sharing hobbies, doing trips or getting over boring lockdown periods. Katrina (Kartofski) was a great discussion partner for many topics and we shared some very cool adventures. The whole team of AV-MAVT (doctoral association) made the PhD years much more colorful. Our common interest in trying to achieve a better and more diverse work environment resulted in many deep or hilarious discussions. Other friends from high school, university or private environments enriched those years with interesting travels, mountain biking and ski-touring trips, festivals or a substantial amount of emptied bottles. I especially would like to thank Susan for her love and support in the final period of my PhD. Last, but not least, I would like to thank my parents Sabine and Jürgen Weichart for all their support over those years, getting me to the point I am now, as well as my siblings.

List of Symbols

Symbol	Description	S.I. Unit
$d_{membrane}$	Membrane diameter	μm
$d_{electrode}$	Electrode diameter	μm
d_{bumper}	Bumper diameter	μm
d_{via}	Via diameter	μm
$h_{membrane}$	Membrane height	μm
$h_{stopper}$	Stopper height	μm
h_{skin}	Silicone skin- height	μm
h_{bump}	Height silicone over sensor	μm
$t_{membrane}$	Thickness membrane	μm
L	Line width electrodes	μm
S	Space between electrodes	μm
$w_{undercut}$	etch undercut	μm
M	Number of fibers	
N	Number of sensors on fiber	
dC_{sensor}	Capacitance change	fF
$R1$	Sensitivity R1	fF/mN
$R2$	Sensitivity R2	fF/mN
S_R	Sensitivity ratio	[ ]
M1	Membrane design	
GEN1	Mask generation	
D1	Device from GEN2	
L1	Layer in fabrication	
EV1	Electronics version	
1S1	Sensor at location 1,1	

List of Abbreviations

Abbrev.	Description	Explanation
1E / 3E	1 / 3 - Electrode	Taxel configuration
ADC	Analog digital converter	
AD2	Analog discovery 2	
BRNC	Binnig & Rohrer Nanotechnology Center	
CAPEX	Capital expenditure	
CTE	Coefficient of thermal expansion	
DAC	Digital analog converter	
DL	Device left	Type of sensing array (GEN3)
DR	Device right	Type of sensing array (GEN3)
FC	Force-capacitance	Plot type
FD	Force-displacement	Plot type
FFC	Flexible flat cable	Connector type
FFT	Fast fourier transform	
FIB	Focused ion beam	Measurement tool
FO	Fan-Out	Packaging technology
FPGA	Field programmable gate array	
GUI	Graphical user interface	
IC	Integrated circuit	
ICP	Inductively coupled plasma	Plasma processing method
L/S	Line and space	Width and distance of electrodes
LDV	Laser doppler vibrometer	Measurement tool
MEMS	Micro-Electro Mechanical System	
OFET	Organic field effect transistor	
OPEX	Operational expenditure	
PI	Polyimide	
RDL	Redistribution layer	Wiring layers in a substrate
RIE	Reactive ion etch	Processing tool
RMS	Root Mean Square	

RSD	Relative standard deviation	
SEM	Scanning electron microscopy	
SNR	Signal to noise ratio	
Std	Standard deviation	
Taxel	Tactile cell, Tactile sensor	
TIA	Transimpedance amplifier	
WiW	Within wafer	Uniformity criterium
WLI	White light interferometry	Measurement tool
WtW	Wafer to wafer	Uniformity criterium

Contents

Contents

List of Figures

List of Tables

1 Introduction

1.1 Preamble

Some publications were written in the course of this doctoral thesis, which summarize well the performed activities. Significant parts of the text in this thesis were taken and adapted from those publications. For the sake of readability the sections are not marked. Where applicable, it is however mentioned which results corresponded to which publications. The introduction and motiviation of the work was introduced in [1, 2].

1.2 Motivation

Humans have remarkable capabilities for exploring and interacting with objects due to their tactile sense. Improving this sense in robots can increase their dexterity [3, 4] or give prostheses the sense of touch [5]. The fingertips are the most important part for exploration and classification tasks. The focus of this thesis is to investigate the possibility to design an artificial fingertip with similar sensing capabilities and a similar form factor as the human counterpart. The aim is to replicate the human sense of touch through advanced sensing technology.

1.3 The human tactile sense

The skin in the fingertip comprises of four different tactile cells for mechanical stimuli, their capabilities are shown in Table 1.1. This thesis focuses on the tactile sensing capabilities for mechanical stimuli in a human fingertip, where the density of tactile receptors is the highest [6]. They are capable of sensing static and dynamic touch in a range of 1-10 kPa (Meissner and Merkel endings), detect strain in the skin (Ruffini endings) as well as perceive vibrations of up to 500 Hz (Pacini endings). The density of touch sensing cells is the highest with about 1 sensor / mm^2, followed by a lower density of strain & vibration sensing cells [6, 7].

Table 1.1: Summary of the capabilities of mechanic tactile senses in the human finger skin [6–9].

Sense	FA-I **Dynamic Touch**	SA-I **Static Touch**	FA-II **Vibration Sensing**	SA-II **Strain sensing**
Name	Meissner endings	Merkel endings	Pacini endings	Ruffini endings
Density [#/cm²]	70-140	70	20	10
Frequency range [Hz]	5-50	5	40-400	5
Sensitivity [Pa]	Min 700-1300	Max 10kPa		
Sensitivity deformation [µm]	6	30	0.08	300
Density maps				

Fig. 1.1 gives an overview on the core elements of a human finger. The key features are its softness for delicate object interaction, small size, and durability against mechanical damage. This allows for conformity, effective exploration and interaction.

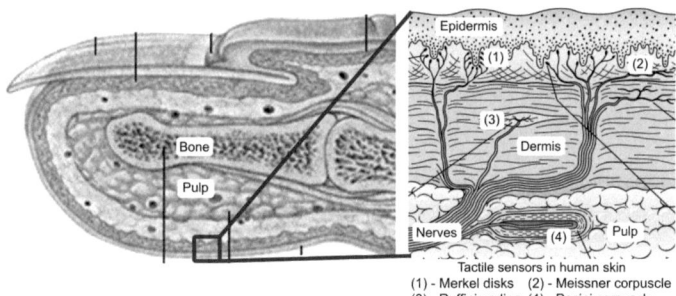

Tactile sensors in human skin
(1) - Merkel disks (2) - Meissner corpuscle
(3) - Ruffini ending (4) - Pacini corpuscle

Figure 1.1: Overview on the human fingertip and its tactile senses, adapted from [10, 11].

1.4 Research objective & state of the art

The overall goal of this thesis is to explore a tactile sensing technology which can replicate the human tactile sense in a fingertip. Table 1.2 summarizes the criteria for such a sensing technology. The sensing requirements originate from human sensing capabilities, assuming those capabilities can be seen as a gold standard. Integration and reliability criteria are defined to allow a broad usability of the technology in potential robotic or prosthetic applications and are partially connected to the human counterpart. The existing technologies are explained in more detail in the next section.

Table 1.2: Criteria and goals for an artificial fingertip. The pro's and con's of existing technologies are summarized, details are in section 1.4.1.

	Criteria	Range/Goal	Indirect - BioTac	Indirect - Camera based	Indirect - Magnetic flux based	Direct - conductive fiber crossbars	Direct - Sensing skins
	References		[15]	[17-21]	[22-24]	[25-27]	[9,28-33]
Sensing	Pressure Range	1 - 10 kPa	Not specified, plausible	Proven	Not specified, plausible	Not specified, general lower	Proven
	Spatial resolution	1 mm touch, 3 mm vibration	Coarser (19 electrodes on finger)	Proven	Not specified, plausible	Coarser	Proven
	Frequency range	0-500 Hz	Proven (1 sensor only)	Limited in detecting very small deformations and high frequency signals			Proven
	Strain / Shear sensing	No quantitative data for humans	Proven (measures full finger deformation)	Proven (measures full finger)	Proven (measures full finger)	Mainly pressure sensing	Proven
Integration	Integration 3D finger	Applicability to human sized finger (L/W/H = 25/15/10 mm)	Bigger due to peripheral components and sensors	Downsizing difficult due to camera and optical path	Proven	Downsizing difficult	Not investigated
	Compliance	Human-like	Plausible	Plausible	Plausible	Plausible	Not investigated
	Electrical interfaces	Reliability and simplicity	Plausible	Proven	Proven	Proven, manual connections	Partially studied
	Manufacturing and Cost	Minimized	Expensive, 15k $ per finger	Some open-source projects claim low price, DIGIT 300$	Good, commercial Hall sensors available	Low	Not investigated
Reliability	Mechanical Robustness	Application dependent, no standards	Metrics not defined	Metrics not defined	Metrics not defined	Metrics not defined	Metrics not defined
	Susceptibility to noise	No crosstalk from electromagnetic (EM) /thermal noise, no drift	Limited (thermal drift)	Good	Unclear behavior in EM noisy environments	Low shielding in noisy (EM/thermal) environments.	Depends on technology

1.4.1 Existing solutions

Various solutions have been developed to replicate the human tactile sense. They are structured here into two main groups, indirect and direct sensing solutions:

1. Indirect sensing: measurement of the deformation of a whole body, such as the artificial fingertip. Indirect sensing solutions have reached a higher level of maturity at this point in time.

2. Direct sensing: measurement with arrays of tactile sensors (taxels) or cross-junctions on a surface, which is more comparable with the sensing principle in the human skin.

There are several reviews on tactile sensing technologies (e.g. [7,12–14]), this work only summarizes a few important examples and more recent results in Table 1.2:

- **BioTac by SynTouch [15] (indirect):** reached market-readiness and includes an array of 19 electrodes for touch measurement as well as one pressure sensor for vibration measurement. The devices are used in humanoid robotic hands as fingertip sensors [16].

- **Camera-based sensing systems (indirect):** studied in several approaches like DIGIT [17], GelSight [18], Omnitact [19], by Sferazza et al. [20] or a thumb sized model proposed by Sun et al. [21]. Those camera-based sensing systems are popular in many robotic research groups, particularly due to the straight-forward applicability of vision-based evaluation software and neural networks, which are researched in many robotic groups. The presented solutions were used to extract features like contact forces & locations, or to classify objects.

- **Magnetic flux sensing systems (indirect):** magnetic based soft tactile sensors [22–24] use arrays of Hall sensors to measure the location shift of magnetic particles in a soft body.

- **Conductive-fiber based (direct):** crossbar matrices of conducting fibers with a resistive [25,26] or insulating (measuring capacitance) [27] interposer layer. Those sensors are easy to fabricate and hereby allowed a simple transfer to robotic testing environments. They are a very promising technology for measuring touch over larger areas.

- **Sensing skins (direct):** Many groups worked on advanced sensing skins with higher spatial resolution, more sensing capabilities or higher

5

sensitivities, a small overview is listed here. Oh et al. [28] used ZnO based piezoelectric thin film transistor (TFT) arrays for force and shear force measurements while Boutry et al. [9] addressed this task with a grid of carbon nanotube based electrodes. Lee et al. [29] built arrays of direction-sensitive tactile sensors by using four electrodes below a PDMS bump while Liang et al. [30] used a similar approach with an interposer layer consisting of truncated pyramids for higher sensitivity. Chun et al. [31] combined two sensing layers (resistive graphene sensing array & triboelectric sensing layer) for touch and vibration measurements with high spatial resolution. Someya et al. [32] presented pressure sensor arrays based on a resistive sensing principle, directly amplified by an organic field effect transistor (OFET), while Zhu et al. [33] use a capacitive element for measuring coupled with an OFET. Further work presents the integration of commercial sensors in a fingertip like Schmitz et al. [34] who covered a finger with 12 capacitive sensors.

1.4.2 White spots & research goal

Table 1.3 summarizes the weak spots of the existing technologies. The more advanced indirect solutions have systematic drawbacks, which might ultimately limit their applicability. Sensing skins on the other side were proven to have good sensing capabilities, based on various sensing principles.

Table 1.3: Weak spots of existing sensing technologies.

Technology	References	Drawbacks
BioTac finger	[15]	Lacks spatial resolution & downsizing capability.
Camera-based sensing systems	[17–21]	Limited in vibration detection and downsizing capability.
Magnetic flux sensing systems	[22–24]	Limited in vibration detection, unclear behavior in environments with electromagnetic noise.
Cross-bar fiber networks	[25–27]	Limited downsizing capabilities (alignment of fibers), incompressible interposer materials result in lower sensitivities, longer time-constants for deformation and relaxation (dynamic sensing limited), temperature cross-sensitivity (especially for resistive interposers).
Sensing skins	[9, 28–33]	Integration/robustness to be studied.

The aim of this thesis is to explore a solution for a sensing skin, which allows the integration into a human-sized fingertip and fulfills the defined criteria in Table 1.2. Hereby, the conceptual advantages of good sensing capabilities and flexible & compact integration shall be harvested. The following questions need to be answered for this:

- How can we improve the integration flexibility of two-dimensional sensing skins? Is it possible to address this with only a flexible substrate or are flexible and stretchable substrates necessary? The latter strongly limits the scope of possible materials and minimum feature sizes [35].

- What type of taxel is ideally used for the envisioned applications?

- Does the new concept allow a compact finger-sized integration and is it robust enough while still fulfilling all sensing requirements?

1.5 Sensing concept

A concept drawing of the proposed artificial fingertip is shown in Fig. 1.2 and described in patent application [36]. It consists of three major components:

1. Simplified finger consisting of the backbone, pulp (a soft filler material) as well as the sturdy bulk.

2. Fiber based sensing array with the potentially integrated circuits (IC's).

3. Skin layer for protecting the sensors.

The main ideas behind this approach are:

- The usage of 1D fibers, which are like nerve fibers in a human, allow an easy integration of taxels in a 3D body. The fibers in this work are a simple array of straight fibers, but arbitrary shapes or splitting fibers are possible to cover 3D bodies more efficiently.

- The sensing fibers are placed in a sturdy outer layer of silicone which surrounds the soft, inner pulp. Hereby a soft finger can be built using a thin, robust silicone layer which achieves softness through its low thickness. This is advantageous over a homogenous body, which would need to consist of much softer material (with often worse material properties) to achieve similar mechanical characteristics.

7

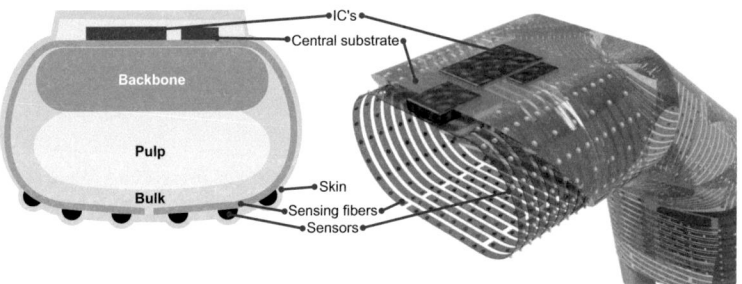

Figure 1.2: Overview on the artificial fingertip and its main components. [2]

This approach allows the usage of flexible materials with limited stretchability and hereby more design flexibility for the taxels. The overall limitation of sensing skins with stretchable materials is that many miniaturization techniques are limited, like the patterning width of electrodes or features [35]. Several of the proposed taxel architectures are based on stretchable electrodes (e.g. [9]), which can be downscaled to minimum feature sizes of around 150 μm with state-of-the-art technologies [37], limiting the amount of electrodes in the 1D fibers significantly . Others use conductive metal layers on stretchable substrates (e.g. [29–31]), which are prone to degradation upon mechanical deformation [38,39]. Further solutions use meandering structures to maintain low stress in metallic traces, which however need large surface areas or 3D features [35,40,41]. Many of the proposed designs will therefore not justify the needs of a robust, integrable sensing technology.

There are multiple possible approaches for the design of the taxels. The most relevant technologies from the previous section are evaluated here and their sensing capabilities are compared to the chosen design later in Table 2.17:

- Capacitive: many sensor designs are based on this principle, e.g. [9, 29, 30, 33]. The basic principle of two conducting layers and a compressible, insulating interposer can be realized with many fabrication techniques, allowing design and material choice flexibility. A soft and compressible interposer allows for higher sensitivity. This can for example be compressible structured layers [9, 30] or an air gap [29]. Capacitive sensing solutions show little sensitivity to temperature changes.

- Piezoresistive: this technology is also widely used, and the insulating interposer of the capacitor is replaced with a resistive layer, which changes its resistance upon compression. This was for example implemented by [26, 31, 32, 42, 43]. Temperature cross-sensitivity of the resistance can be reduced by designs which modify the contact resistance rather than the bulk resistance [31]. Such a structured resistive interposer layer however is often more complex to form and suspected to be less reliable upon the application of shear forces on the material stack. Resistive measurement approaches have the advantage of easier readout electronics.

- Piezoelectric: this approach was for example used by [28, 44]. It shows promising sensing capabilities, design and process flow are however strongly coupled to the piezoelectric material chosen and necessitate detailed process know-how.

- Combination with OFET's: OFET's allow the direct amplification of sensor signals, hereby increasing signal gain and potentially reduce the signal-to-noise (SNR) ratio [32, 33]. This approach as well needs detailed processing-knowhow on the organic semiconducting material.

- Other approaches are pyrolectric layers [31], conductive-fluid-based architectures [45, 46], magnetic film or permanent magnet-based [22, 24], or with even other measurement principles (compare the reviews [7, 12–14]).

Capacitive sensing technology with an air gap is used in this thesis for the following expected advantages:

- Easy integration in the planned flexible substrate process with standard materials.

- Small possible form factor of the taxel unit.

- High sensitivity possible by using a very narrow air gap, which is easily compressible. The sensitivity S is broadly defined as

$$S = \frac{\Delta \; Electrical \; signal}{\Delta \; Applied \; stimulus} \tag{1.1}$$

with the stimulus being the applied force or pressure, if not specified differently.

- No soft/viscoelastic interposer material, which would result in weaker vibration sensing capabilities.

9

- Low temperature cross-sensitivity.

- Reasonable signal strength possible, no direct amplifier stage needed at the sensor.

The taxel design is introduced in detail in chapter 2.

1.6 Thesis outline

This thesis is structured into four chapters:

- Sensing technology: describes the details of the sensing technology, the taxels, cleanroom fabrication as well as taxel characterization.

- Sensor packaging in soft material: presents the packaging of the taxels in a silicone skin, including the evaluation of the sensing characteristics.

- Artificial fingertip: describes the fabrication of an artificial fingertip, the integration of the sensing arrays on this fingertip as well as the characterization of those sensing fingers.

- Characterization setup & electronics: Many of the characterizations presented in this thesis were executed on a dedicated characterization setup. This setup is described, including the readout electronics used for the measurements.

2 Sensing technology

This chapter describes the sensing technology in detail. The device design, fabrication and device generations are introduced. The results contain process characterizations, the appearance of sensors as well as mechanical and electromechanical characterizations. This is followed by an investigation of the manufacturing costs. Significant parts of this chapter were presented in published works [1, 47].

2.1 Device design

The process and device design builds on redistribution layer (RDL) technology (see section 2.2.1) to form an interconnection substrate and integrates additional process steps for creating suspended membranes for capacitive sensing. The direct fabrication of sensors on the substrate should shorten the overall process, allow better miniaturization and avoid complications with the integration of external components, e.g. localized mechanical stresses and potential failure points at the interface between dissimilar materials.

Arrays of sensors allow distributed sensing as depicted in Fig. 2.1A. Polyimide fibers with integrated electrical connections are routed to a multitude of sensors. The sensor arrays are discussed in more detail in section 2.1.4; the single taxels are introduced first.

2.1.1 Taxel design

Fig. 2.1B shows a simplified overview of the proposed sensor while Table 2.1 gives an overview on all positions in the graph.

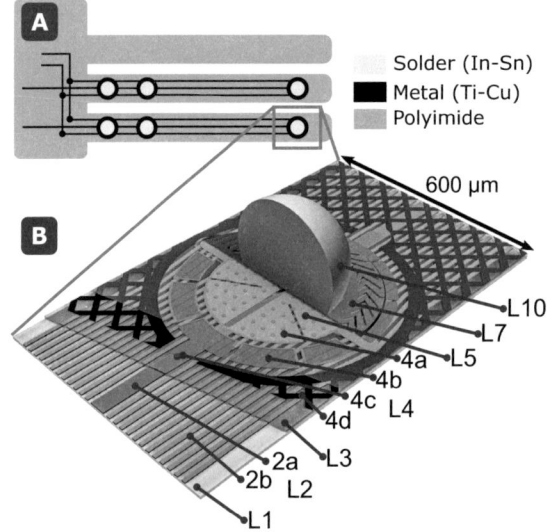

Figure 2.1: A: Overview of the proposed sensor array. B: Taxel with its main structural layers. Adapted from [1].

Table 2.1: Main layers in the taxel. Layers L6, L8 & L9 are only relevant in the fabrication flow discussed later (Fig. 2.7). Adapted from [1].

Nr.	Description	Material	t [μm]
1	Base layer	Polyimide	7.5
2	Wiring layer		
a	Supply line (red)	Metal (Ti-Cu)	1
b	Readout lines (blue)		
3	Interconnection layer	Polyimide	7.5
4	Electrode layer		
a	Electrodes		
b	Membrane Anchors	Metal (Ti-Cu)	1
c	Vias		
d	Shielding grid		
5	Stopper layer	Polyimide	1
7	Membrane layer	Metal (Ti-Cu-Au)	1
10	Bumper	Solder (In-Sn)	210

The device consists of a multi-layer stack of polyimide layers and metal layers, which are used as interconnections. The lowest metal layer is the wiring layer (L2) on which the majority of electrical connections to the sensors are placed. The supply line (2a) is marked in red, the readout lines (2b) going to the different electrodes are marked in blue. Line and space (L/S, L = width of the electrodes, S = space between two electrodes) distance is an important design criterion for the overall array design. It is mainly limited by the processing capabilities as summarized in section 2.4.1. The wiring layer is sandwiched between two thick polyimide layers (L1 & L3).

The second metal layer is the electrode layer (L4), which consists of the readout electrodes (4a, blue), the membrane anchors (4b, red), vias to the wiring layer (4c), the shielding grid (4d, black) along the sensor wires and rerouting connections on the center part of the device. The readout electrode (4a) is either one electrode (1E) for optimal sensitivity or it is split into three individually addressable electrodes (3E). 1E taxels allow the measurement of z-axis static and dynamic forces, while 3E taxels additionally allow force measurements in x and y direction (shear). Such taxels, however, need three times as many electrodes, reducing the overall amount of taxels possible in the array.

A thin polyimide protection layer (L5) is used on one hand to protect the wiring, on the other hand as mechanical end stoppers to avoid the complete pull in of the membrane onto the electrodes. When a force is applied to deform the membrane this first results in a range of high sensitivity due to the deformation of the soft membrane. As soon as the membrane is in contact with the stopper layer, minor deformation results in a larger measurement range and a low sensitivity region of the sensor. The last metal layer is the membrane layer (L7) which hovers over the electrodes, suspended by a ring of springs, which are attached to the membrane anchors. This attachment results from the direct sputtering of L7 onto the membrane anchors of L4. On top of the membrane, a solder bump (L10) is placed. The ball results in a stiffened membrane, and thereby in a flat reference plane over the electrodes.

2.1.2 Device dimensions

Fig. 2.2 shows the most important dimensions of the final device. The complete taxel has a maximum dimension of 0.5 mm, allowing sensor arrays with a spatial resolution below 1 mm. Table 2.2 summarizes the other dimensions for GEN2 & GEN3 taxels. Those generations are introduced later in section 2.3.

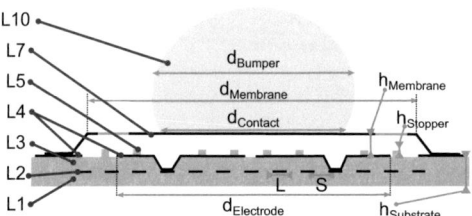

Figure 2.2: Cross section of the taxel with the most important geometric features. Adapted from [1].

Table 2.2: Most important dimensions of the taxel. Empty cells mean that the values were not adapted.

Parameter	GEN2	GEN3	Description
	µm	µm	
$d_{electrode}$	350	390	Electrode diameter.
$d_{membrane}$	440		Membrane diameter
$d_{contact}$	240 - 290	290	240 for M2 & M3, 290 for M1 & M4 (see Fig. 2.3)
d_{bumper}	290		Bumper diameter (sphere with flat or half sphere)
$h_{substrate}$	15		Substrate thickness
$h_{membrane}$	4		Height membrane (largest membrane distance)
$h_{stoppers}$	1		Height stoppers (lowest membrane distance)
L	10 - 20	20	Line width electrodes
S	10 - 20	20	Space between electrodes

2.1.3 Membrane, stopper and bumper design

In the course of this thesis a variety of designs were tested, which are shortly summarized here.

- Membrane / cutout design: The shape of the cut-outs influences the stiffness of the membranes.

- Bumper design: While the volume/diameter of the bumper had no significant influence on the static sensing behavior, the diameter of the contact $d_{contact}$ (see Fig. 2.2) influences the membrane stiffness.

- Stopper design: The modification of the stopper design allowed the tuning of the low-sensitivity region to a certain extent. This effect is explained in section 2.4.4.

Fig. 2.3 depicts the four membrane-bumper designs studied in this work. Two methods modify the stiffness of the membranes. A larger $d_{contact}$ (M1/M4 vs. M2/M3) increases the stiffness of the membrane due to a shorter free length of the spring structures. A larger amount of cut-outs (type M3 vs. M2) decreases the membrane stiffness due to decreased bending stiffness of the folded beams. The mechanic behavior and fabrication reliability of M1 - M3 is evaluated in section 2.4.3, resulting in the selection of M4 for GEN3 devices.

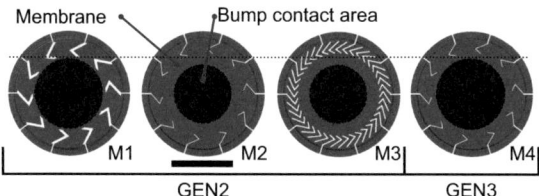

Figure 2.3: Membrane designs M1 - M4 tested in this work. The spring geometries and the bump contact diameter $d_{dContact}$ vary. Drawings to scale (scale bar 250 µm). Adapted from [1].

Those design parameters lost most of their relevance with the silicone coating of the sensors introduced in section 3.3.3. Especially thicker silicone coatings influence the mechanical behavior more than the thin metal membrane.

2.1.4 Array design

Fig. 2.4A shows an overview of a sensor array with 12 x 12 sensors and a spacing of 1 x 1 mm. Counting of sensors always starts in the lower left corner of the array. The taxels are coded as mSn with m = fiber/column number and n = sensor/row number along the fiber.

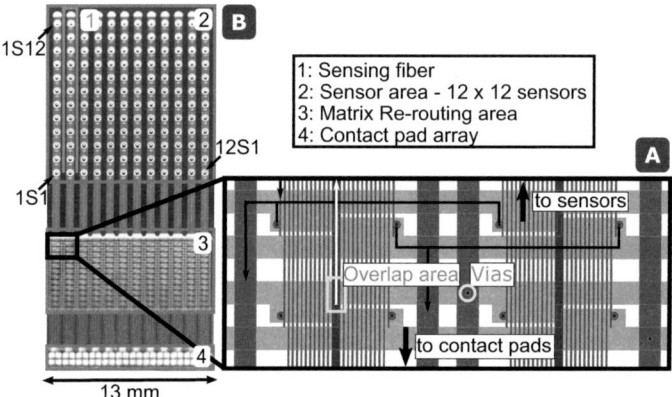

Figure 2.4: A: Photograph of a sensing array. B: Detail of the matrix re-routing area. Supply lines are red, readout lines are blue, vias are black dots. The signal flow is marked with white (supply) and black (readout) arrows. Adapted from [1].

The interconnects to the sensors are re-routed in the matrix re-routing field as highlighted in Fig. 2.4B. The signal goes along the power lines (in red, white arrow) towards the sensing array and returns on one of the signal lines (in blue). Horizontal wires connect all sensors of the same index to one common readout line as highlighted by the black arrows. The overlap area between power and signal lines is kept small to reduce the capacitance $C_{Rerouting}$ (see section 2.1.5). The M (amount of sensing fibers) x N (amount of sensors per fiber) sensors are hereby connected to M + N contact pads at the bottom of the device. Those contact pads can be interfaced to readout any sensor independently in the array.

The design incorporates a relatively large distance of 12.5 mm between the sensing array and the contact pads for two reasons:

1. The length of parallel conductors should be representative to the lengths in a final device to have comparable electrical characteristics.

2. This setup facilitates the testing of the sensor arrays as the contact pads are easier accessible.

The whole design, including the matrix re-routing area, can be significantly miniaturized when needed. 100 μm line width of all features is kept for maximum fabrication reliability, not due to electrical constraints as discussed in the next section.

2.1.5 Electrical readout and scalability

Relative range A schematic of the readout electronics for the sensor array is presented in Fig. 2.5 to enable a scalability analysis. The sensor array is essentially a capacitive cross bar matrix. A signal is applied to power line m and the output signal is acquired via readout line n, and amplified by a charge amplifier. The measured capacitance $C_{m,n}$ consists of

$$C_{m,n} = C_{Rerouting} + C_{Sensor} \tag{2.1}$$

with the following values (for GEN3):

1. The re-routing capacitance $C_{Rerouting} = 7.7fF$ comes from the overlap area as defined in Fig. 2.4 and only occurs once for each sensor (hereby not influencing scalability). Any other overlap area relates to another measured capacitance $C_{!m,n}$ (all taxels with other indexes than m,n).

2. The sensor capacitance $C_{Sensor} = \frac{\epsilon A}{z}$ is defined by the dimensions in Fig. 2.1 and results in $C_{Sensor,0} = 261fF$ and $C_{Sensor,max} = 1046fF$.

This results in a relative range of

$$R_{rel} = \frac{\Delta C}{C_{Rerouting} + C_{Sensor,0}} \tag{2.2}$$

which should be as large as possible to allow best possible resolution and a highest possible Signal to Noise Ratio (SNR) with the connected readout electronics. It is independent of the array size.

17

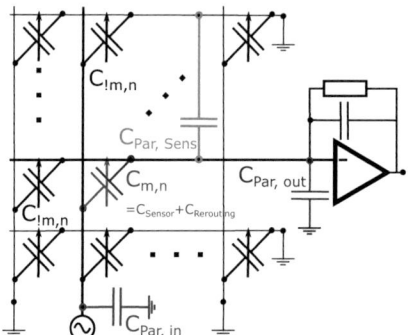

Figure 2.5: Electrical schematics of the readout, showing a simplified sensor network and a connected charge amplifier. Adapted from [1].

Parasitic capacitances The parasitic capacitances to ground do not influence the relative range of the sensors, they however need to be driven by the power supply respectively by the amplifier circuit. For large sensing networks this results in a higher power consumption and, depending on the chosen components, it influences the noise levels and amplifier circuit stability.

The shielding grid around the wirings (depicted in Fig. 2.1, 4d) and around the re-routing area induces the parasitic capacitances $C_{par,in}$ and $C_{par,out}$ to ground. Additionally, $C_{par,sens}$ describes the capacitance between parallel sensor lines, which adds up to the capacitance to ground, as the inactive power and readout lines are on ground potential while the active sensor is read out. The same is valid for all not-measured capacitances $C_{!m,n}$. This results in the following total parasitic capacitances:

$$
\begin{aligned}
C_{par,IN} &= C_{par,in} + C_{par,sens} + C_{Sensor} \cdot N \\
&= 2\epsilon l_{fiber} \cdot \left(\frac{L_{Power} f_{coverage}}{t_{PI}} + \frac{t_{signal}}{S} \right) + C_{Sensor} \cdot N
\end{aligned}
\tag{2.3}
$$

$$
\begin{aligned}
C_{par,OUT} &= (C_{par,out,fiber} + C_{par,sens} + C_{Sensor}) \cdot M \\
&= \left(2\epsilon l_{fiber} \cdot \left(\frac{L f_{coverage}}{t_{PI}} + \frac{t_{signal}}{S} \right) + C_{Sensor} \right) \cdot M
\end{aligned}
\tag{2.4}
$$

with all variables described in Table 2.3.

Table 2.3: Variables in the parasitic capacitance calculation

Variable	Description
ϵ	permittivity of PI
l_{fiber}	Length of sensing fibers
t	thickness of PI / signal wire
$f_{coverage}$	Coverage percentage of the shielding grid
L/S	Line / Space width electrodes
M/N	Total number of fibers / sensors

Table 2.4 contains the calculated parasitic capacitances for GEN3 as well as potential future designs (FD) with longer fibers and 24 x 24 taxels. L/S should be reduced in a final design, not only to allow more sensors per fiber, but also to reduce the parasitic capacitance. Two further approaches exist to reduce the parasitics, if necessary:

1. Thicker PI layers increase the distance to the shielding grid.

2. Reduced coverage of the shielding grid around the electrodes, which however might result in a larger level of extrinsic noise influencing the signal.

Table 2.4: Parasitic capacitances to ground depending for GEN3 and possible future designs (FD).

Design	l_{fiber}	L/S	L_{power}	$f_{coverage}$	M/N	$C_{par,IN}$	$C_{par,OUT}$
	mm	μm	μm		#	pF	pF
GEN 3	18.5	20	40	0.8	12	8.9	38.3
FD 1	35.0	20	40	0.8	24	17.4	139.0
FD 2	35.0	10	40	0.8	24	17.4	76.5

The actual hard limits of the readout electronics are not known and depend on the readout method, but lower parasitic capacitances will simplify the design of a dedicated readout IC.

Allowable line resistances The line resistance is defined by the dimensions of the electrodes with (Ti conductivity is neglected):

$$R_L = \frac{\rho_{Cu} l_{fiber}}{t_{Cu} L}. \tag{2.5}$$

The sensor network can be further simplified to one transmission line and the line resistances included as shown in Fig. 2.6 (details on the PCB electronics are discussed in Fig. 5.8). LT spice simulations showed that line resistances $R_L = R_{in} = R_{out} > 10\ k\Omega$ have an impact on the signal strength. Assuming $l_{fiber} = 35\ mm$ in a future design this would allow a minimum $L \approx 60\ nm$, which is far below the possible fabrication limit discussed in section 2.4.1. On the other hand, 10 µm L/S would allow a maximum fiber length of $l_{fiber} \approx 5.9\ m$, which is much bigger than any reasonable design.

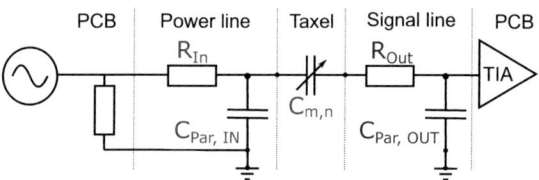

Figure 2.6: Electrical schematic - simplified transmission line of one taxel in the readout.

2.2 Fabrication

Redistribution layer (RDL) technology is used to build up a flexible substrate and a new, RDL-compatible post-process is introduced which allows the fabrication of suspended sensing structures directly on top of this substrate. A sensing technology, compatible with RDL technology and its fabrication lines, allows upscaling to large area and cost-efficient sensing arrays.

2.2.1 Related work in flexible substrate technology

RDL technology is a comprehensive term for a damascene of metal interconnections and insulator layers, used in many industries and technologies (partially under different names, e.g. interposer). Polymers are employed to achieve flexibility. Such RDL's are prominent in modern packaging industry like FanOut (FO) architectures which are discussed in detail in [48]. Some examples are Infineon's FO technology [49] licensed by several large companies in the industry as well as TSMC's integrated FO package [50]. Significant efforts were conducted to implement this technology as well on larger substrates as shown by Fraunhofer [51], Samsung [52] or at Evatec [53]. On the other hand PCB manufacturers try to downscale their feature sizes as presented by Hightec [54] for flexible PCB's. Roll-to-roll processing [55] can achieve even larger scales of fabrication. So far RDL technologies have been mainly used for packaging of conventional silicon MEMS as presented in [56, 57] or the integration by soldering of conventional sensors on a flexible substrate as presented by Tomo et al. [22]. Neural implant research is another research area where flexible substrate technology is often found. Fiber-like structures for neural interfaces are for example found in [58–61].

Principally most of the proposed fabrication flows could be used to build up the flexible substrate. As processing details are rarely given and the most limiting factor is the availability of the processing machinery, the process flow in this work had to be adapted. It is closest comparable with the flex-PCB technology in [54] or neural interfaces in [59, 61], however with smaller feature sizes.

2.2.2 Material choice

Table B.1 gives an overview on material properties of the materials considered for the fabrication of the device. Table 2.5 explains the reasons for the finally chosen materials.

Table 2.5: Material choice for the fabrication of the sensing arrays.

Part	Material	Reason
Carrier substrate	Si wafer	Wide availability, machine compatibility
Polymer	PI 26xx	Good mechanical and chemical characteristics, good vacuum processing capability, leveling capability (non-conformal coating), low coefficient of thermal expansion (CTE)
Metal wiring	Ti / Cu (/Au)	Cheap, good availability, low layer stress, good adhesion to polymer (Ti). Au only as thin cover layer.

2.2.3 Fabrication process

Fig. 2.7 summarizes the three main stages in the fabrication process. The full process flow consists of 130 process steps with ten structured layers. The majority of process steps is however needed to build the flexible interconnection substrate. The three stages are explained as:

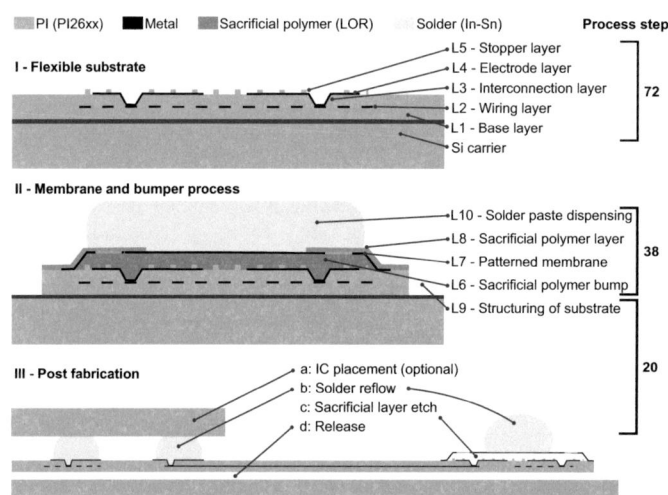

Figure 2.7: Fabrication flow divided into three main stages, showing layers L1 - L10. The amount of process steps per stage is given. Adapted from [1].

1. **Stage I**: the flexible substrate is fabricated as a repetitive process of polyimide (PI) layers and metal interconnections. The PI26xx family by HD Microsystems is used, different viscosities achieve thick (L1 & 3) and thin (L5) layers. Structuring of the PI is done via ICP etching with via sizes down to 5 µm. The metal layers are sputtered Ti-Cu layers, which are structured with wet etching. The wiring layer was successfully tested down to 10 µm L/S distance as discussed in section 2.4.1.

2. **Stage II**: The membrane and bumper process uses RDL compatible processes with slight adaptions. Newly introduced is a sacrificial polymer (LOR 30B, MicroChem) which is used for two purposes. In L6 the polymer forms a bump over the electrodes which will define the three dimensional shape of the membrane. In L8 the sacrificial polymer is used as a masking layer to define the final shape of the solder ball through different surface wettability. The membrane (L7) is a sputtered Ti-Cu-Au layer, structured again with wet etching. After building the complete substrate stack, another plasma etching process (L9) structures the RDL layer stack and separates the fibers. Finally, the solder paste (L10) is dispensed with a stencil process.

3. **Stage III**: In the post fabrication steps, IC's can be placed on the solder pads to form a connection via a ball grid array. So far, this process is not integrated as no dedicated IC is available. The solder paste is reflow-soldered to form possible solder connections to a chip and the bumpers on the membranes. The shape of the bumper can vary from a thin cap to an almost round ball, depending on the desired application. The amount of dispensed solder as well as the size of the pad opening in the sacrificial polymer define the shape. The final steps are the etching of all sacrificial polymer layers to release the membranes as well as the release from the carrier substrate, which is possible either way around. A KOH-based wet etching process dissolves the sacrificial layers while not attacking any other layer. The small contact area between the membrane and the stopper layer (L5) reduces sticking and the membrane spring stiffness overcomes the small residual force, resulting in suspended membranes. No critical point drying is necessary; a simple air-drying process is sufficient. The sensing arrays are released by mechanically peeling them off the carrier. This process, when executed properly, has a 100% yield of working sensors.

2.2.4 Tools

The fabrication of the devices was executed in the Binnig und Rohrer Nanotechnology Center (BRNC), a shared cleanroom facility of ETH Zurich and IBM Research Zurich. Table 2.6 summarizes the used machines. Repeating process steps reduce the overall amount of necessary tools.

Table 2.6: Processing tools

Process	Tools
Sputtering	Von Ardenne multi-chamber sputter tool (Fig. 2.8a)
Wet etching	Wet benches glass beakers
Polymer application and curing	Spin coater & reflow oven
Polymer structuring	Oxford Inductively Coupled Plasma (ICP) source (Fig. 2.8b)
Photolithography	Spin coater, Suss MA6 mask aligner

(a) Multi-chamber sputter tool   (b) ICP etch tool

Figure 2.8: Photos of the cleanroom process tools

2.3 Devices and masks

This section gives an overview on the different device generations and masks, which were used in this thesis. They are ordered chronologically and the main intentions behind each mask generation are explained. Appendix A.1 summarizes all devices fabricated in the course of this thesis.

2.3.1 GEN0 - Test structure mask

Fig. 2.9 shows the first mask, which was used for a large amount of process tests. It consists of an alternating pattern of either *pillars and lines* - freestanding structures or *holes and trenches* - enclosed structures. There are different features: long lines in varying distance to each other (space variation), round pillars and rectangular pillars. They are all varied in their critical dimensions between 5 - 600 µm. Despite the simplicity of the mask it was a powerful tool for most initial machine and process characterizations. Analyses could be done on 20 x 20 mm chip level (e.g. after dicing of a patterned test wafer) or over the whole wafer to characterize processing uniformity. The mask will be available in the supplementary data as a GDS file.

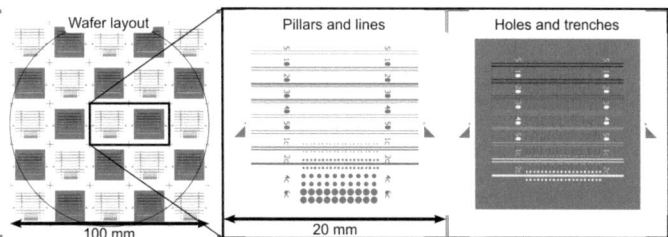

Figure 2.9: Overview on the test structure mask. The 100 mm wafer mask consists of 20 x 20 mm designs of test structures. They are either consisting of *pillars and lines* or *holes and trenches*.

2.3.2 GEN1 - Single taxel process integration

The GEN1 mask was used to test the integration of all process steps of
the taxels onto a flexible substrate. The flexible substrate architecture is
simplified compared to Fig. 2.4 and only a few taxels can be electrically
connected, others could be only optically characterized. Fig. 2.10A shows
a photograph of the 20 x 20 mm chip, which allowed rapid testing of the
process integration steps. Fig. 2.10B-D show the released sensors on a 2
μm thick PI substrate as well as micrographs of initial sensor studies. The
results are not further discussed in the course of this thesis, as they are
outdated. Important studies performed on this device generation were:

- Process integration: simple interconnection substrate, sacrificial layer
  process, membrane process, solder ball generation

- Stopper layer design studies: height, shape

- Membrane design parameter studies: size, height, cut-outs

- Solder ball parameter studies: size, volume, contact area. Fig. 2.10D
  shows for example solder balls of different volume and lower contact
  area

- Mechanical characterization of freestanding membranes.

- First electromechanical characterizations.

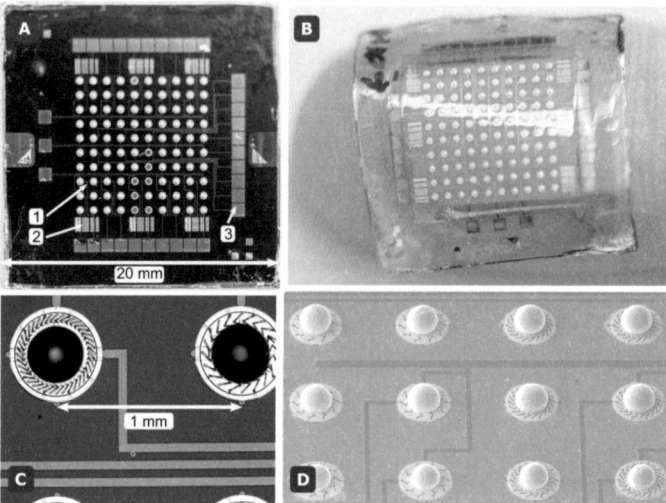

Figure 2.10: Overview GEN1. A: photograph of the 20 x 20 mm chip, with 1 - the sensors, 2 - test structures and 3 - contact pads. B: photograph of the released, 2 μm thick substrate on a human finger. C: microscope picture of two sensors with different membrane designs. D: SEM graph under 45° of sensors with varying membranes and solder balls.

2.3.3 GEN2 - Sensing arrays

This device generation was used for testing the integration of fully functioning sensing arrays into the flexible substrate. Fig. 2.11A shows the 100 mm wafer design with the main structural layers, consisting of five 30 x 30 mm chips as well as four areas of test structures. The test structures are explained later. Each chip contained three devices D1 - D3 summarized in Table 2.7.

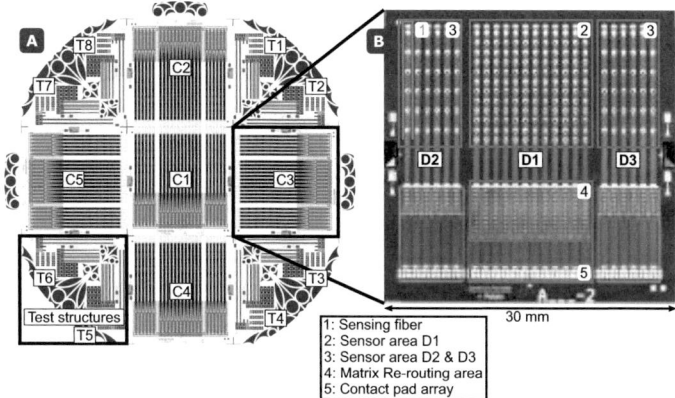

Figure 2.11: Overview GEN2. A: 100 mm wafer mask design with five 30 x 30 mm chips and four test structure areas. Chip indexes C1-5 and test structure indexes T1-8 are marked. B: photograph of one chip with its most important elements. B adapted from [1].

Table 2.7: Devices in GEN2.

Name	L/S [µm]	Electrodes	Array size	Sensor type
D1	10	12 x 24	12 x 12	1E & 3E (alternating)
D2 & D3	20	6 x 12	6 x 6	1E & 3E (alt.)

An important aspect of GEN2 was the testing and validation of the flexible substrate. A variety of test structures was used on the wafer, which are shown in Fig. 2.12. Table 2.8 describes the different components.

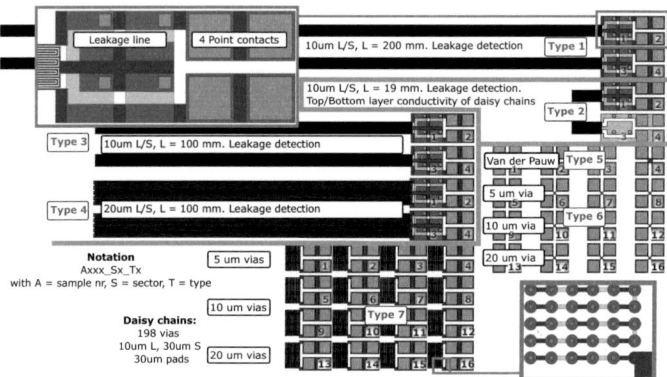

Figure 2.12: Test structures of GEN2 & 3.

Table 2.8: Description of the test structures shown in Fig. 2.12

Type	Description	Tested variations	Measurement results
1 - 4	Line resistance and leakage	10 - 20 µm L/S, 19 - 200 mm length	Very long meandering line to measure the line resistance. The leakage electrode connects to a line between each meander to measure the leakage resistance.
5	Van der Pauw structure	N/A	Measure sheet resistance of metallization layers
6	Single vias for contact resistance	5 - 20 µm via	Contact resistance of one single via from L2 to L4 metallization
7	Daisy chains for contact resistance	5 - 20 µm vias	Contact resistance of 198 daisy-chained vias from L2 to L4 metallization

The devices of GEN2 were used for many tests, particularly all results presented in the publications [1,47] as well as results in this chapter. The most important measurements are summarized as follows:

- Mechanical and electromechanical characterizations of taxels, including 3D sensing capabilities.

- Evaluation of the sensing array: avoidance of crosstalk between sensors.

- Soft material integration: first on-chip studies were performed on this device generation.

2.3.4 GEN3 - Sensing arrays for artificial finger integration

GEN3 devices are similar to GEN2 devices, merely the design of the flexible substrate changed (Fig. 2.13) to build two types of sensing arrays summarized in Table 2.9. Additionally, the membrane design and dimensions were slightly altered as shown in Table 2.2 and Fig. 2.3. The largest difference is the change from the contact pad array to an array of contacts for a flexible flat cable (FFC) connection. This allowed an easier integration of the sensing array with a readout PCB as discussed later in section 4.3. The devices of GEN3 were mainly used for finger integration studies as presented in [2].

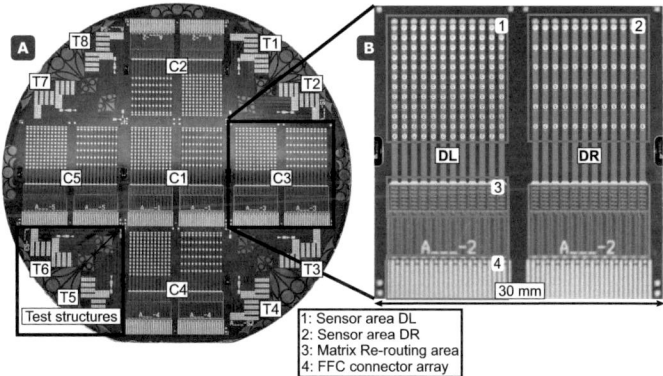

Figure 2.13: Overview GEN3. A: Photograph of a wafer after fabrication (before dicing & solder ball application). Chip indexes C1-5 and test structure indexes T1-8 are marked. B: photograph of one chip with its key elements. B adapted from [2].

Table 2.9: Devices in GEN3.

Name	L/S [µm]	Electrodes	Array size	Sensor type
DL (dev. left)	20	12 x 12	12 x 12	1E
DR (dev. right)	20	12 x 12	12 x 6	1E & 3E (alt.)

2.4 Results

2.4.1 Flexible substrate characterization

Three studies are presented here, which are closely related to the test structures introduced in Fig. 2.12: a line resistance study, a leakage study and a contact resistance study. The device fabrication was partially executed by Ayeshabanu Walikar in the course of the Master thesis project.

2.4.1.1 Line resistance

Test structures of type 3 & 4 (see Fig. 2.12) were used for this study, which consist of 100 mm long meanders with either 10 or 20 μm L/S. The line resistances and leakage currents were measured with compensated probe needles in the electrical probe station in BRNC. Five wafers were fabricated with the first polyimide and wiring layer (L1-L2, compare Fig. 2.1) and the test structures in all sectors were measured. The wafers in this study have a 100 nm Ti layer and a 400-1200 nm Cu layer. Table 2.10 summarizes the average line resistances and relative standard deviations (RSD)

$$RSD = \sigma/\mu * 100 \ [\%] \tag{2.6}$$

with σ being the standard deviation and μ the mean of all measurement data. The data is calculated Within each Wafer (WiW) and across all wafers (Wafer to Wafer - WtW).

Table 2.10: Results of line resistance measurements on five wafers with a 100 nm Ti + 400 nm Cu layer. 128 devices measured.

	10 μm L/S				20 μm L/S			
Sample	WiW - average	WiW - RSD	WtW - average	WtW - RSD	WiW - average	WiW - RSD	WtW - average	WtW - RSD
	Ω	%	Ω	%	Ω	%	Ω	%
Goal	-	<5%	-	<5%	-	<5%	-	<5%
W1	633.1	4.2			266.7	3.0		
W2	637.5	5.6			270.4	4.3		
W3	621.6	5.5	637.6	3.0	268.9	3.1	272.2	3.2
W4	673.6	3.4			289.0	2.4		
W5	622.0	3.6			265.8	2.2		

Fig. 2.14 additionally shows the line resistance averages and error bars versus the four test structure quadrants on all wafers. Counting of the quadrants starts clockwise in the top, right corner as visible in Fig. 2.11. A slightly higher resistance is observable for T1 & T3.

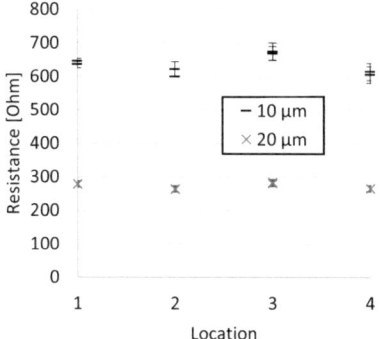

Figure 2.14: Average resistance in T1, T3, T5 & T7 test structure quadrants (see Fig. 2.11).

Similar studies were performed with thicker Cu layers and all data is summarized in Table 2.11. The line resistances for 10 - 20 µm L/S are given and highlighted for 800 nm Cu thickness, which was decided to be the standard design thickness. The mask undercut $w_{undercut}$ (compare Fig. 2.15) is the same for both line widths and can be calculated as

$$R_1 = \frac{C}{L_1 - 2 \cdot w_{undercut}}$$
$$R_2 = \frac{C}{L_2 - 2 \cdot w_{undercut}}$$
$$R_1(L_1 - 2 \cdot w_{undercut}) = R_2(L_2 - 2 \cdot w_{undercut}) \qquad (2.7)$$
$$w_{undercut} = \frac{R_1 L_1 - R_2 L_2}{2 \cdot (R_1 - R_2)}$$

31

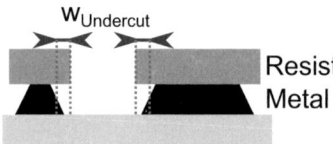

Figure 2.15: Sketch of the undercut in metal etching (not to scale). It is independent of the line width.

with L being the line width (10 or 20 µm), R being the resistance of the lines and $C = \frac{\rho l}{t}$. This study allowed a few important observations, which are relevant for the device understanding:

Table 2.11: Overview of fabrication results for different wiring thickness.

Cu thickness	nm	400	**800**	1200
10 µm - Line res.	Ω / 100 mm	637.6	**336.0**	255.3
20 µm - Line res.	Ω / 100 mm	272.2	**139.2**	96.5
$w_{undercut}$	µm	1.3	**1.5**	2.0

- **Line resistance:** The line resistances are given, which allows the estimation of the total resistance in the final device, depending on the chosen design parameters. The maximum line length for the GEN2 and GEN3 devices is around 20 mm. Resistances to and from the sensors are therefore below 100 Ω and far away from the critical range of $> 10k\Omega$ (see section 2.1.5).

- **Undercut:** The undercut data allows the estimation of the minimum stable line widths. For 800 nm Cu it is 1.5 µm. 5 µm line widths (resulting in finally 2 µm wide lines) would therefore be possible, they are however more sensitive to small process variations.

- **Defect density:** 64 devices per line width were measured in the study presented in Table 2.10. The amount of defect structures was 10 for 10 µm line width and 1 for 20 µm line width. This coincided with the observations of more defect sensing arrays with 10 µm L/S in the GEN2 design. All sensing arrays in GEN3 were therefore adapted to 20 µm L/S. This behavior is related to the defect density in the fabrication, which is directly related to particle defects. A cleaner fabrication environment would greatly improve this behavior and allow finer L/S, and hereby more electrodes per sensing fiber.

- **Fabrication reliability:** The WiW and WtW uniformities presented in Table 2.10 are all around 5% or lower, and are generally better for 20 µm L/S. The resistance variations in the sensing arrays are therefore expected to be small and negligible.

2.4.1.2 Leakage

All test structures described in the previous section were tested for their leakage to the third electrode (compare Fig. 2.12, inset on the top left). All functioning devices showed leakage resistances of 5-10 GΩ for the electrodes running 100 mm in parallel with space distances of 10 - 20 µm. This is the detection limit of the used wafer prober. It therefore could be concluded that the elaborated process is very capable of electrically separating the traces, and a resistive path between the electrodes can be excluded.

This is not the case if particle defects occur, which can result in a shortcut to the leakage electrode. Such particle defects would therefore also connect different readout electrodes and result in measurement errors as later discussed in section 5.4.

2.4.1.3 Contact resistance

Another important element of the flexible substrate are the interconnections between layers, especially through the 7.5 µm thick PI layer (L3 in Fig. 2.1). Three of the wafers introduced in Table 2.10 were additionally fabricated with L3 & L4 and all daisy chain structures (type 7) were measured on those devices. Fig. 2.16 depicts SEM pictures of the fabricated structures and Fig. 2.17 summarizes the results.

Figure 2.16: SEM/FIB images of the daisy chains with 10 µm diameter contacts after the fabrication.

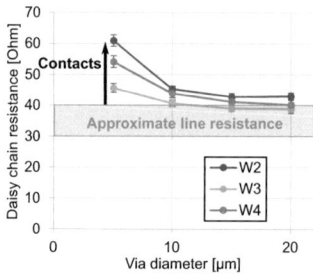

Figure 2.17: Resistance of the daisy chains for different via diameters (5 - 20 μm). 192 devices measured.

The estimation of the line resistance without the contacts is difficult to obtain exactly, as the lines do not have a continuous line width as well as due to current crowding effects [62]. The line resistance approximately lies between 30-40 Ω, and is assumed to be responsible for the majority of the measured resistance for larger vias. The data allows to draw some important conclusions:

- Contact resistance: Assuming that large vias have a very small contact resistance one can observe the difference for the smallest vias versus the biggest vias. This results in an average additional contact of 0.03 - 0.09 Ω per 5 μm via. Such a low contact resistance is very good, also when compared to industrially produced vias [53] (0.02 Ω for 5 μm vias), as the via walls were not specifically tapered or the contact holes filled up with plated metal. The results satisfy the requirements for the proposed sensing array, as only a small amount of vias are placed in the conductive traces to and from the sensors. The additional resistance is negligible compared to the line resistance, and the smallest vias can be used without concerns.

- Process reliability: Only 5 of 192 measured devices (with 198 vias each) showed very high resistances, which could be due to particle defects or a not-opened via. This was independent of the via diameter. The process therefore was judged to be reliable for all via diameters.

- Process repeatability: The WiW uniformity was 2-4%, the WtW uniformity is influenced by the variations in line resistance and therefore more difficult to evaluate. Due to the low impact of the additional resistance this effect was not further investigated.

2.4.2 Appearance

Fig. 2.18 and Fig. 2.19 show SEM pictures of the fabricated sensors. The first picture shows a segment of the fabricated sensor arrays, the second picture is a close-up of one sensor. The images are comparable with the concept picture in Fig. 2.1. The wiring layer (L2) is covered by the polyimide, the electrode (L4) and membrane layer (L7) are however well visible.

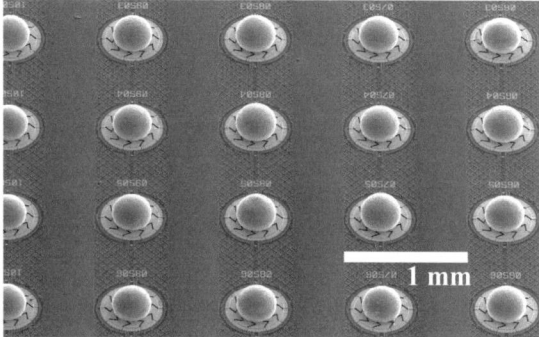

Figure 2.18: SEM picture of a sensor array. [1]

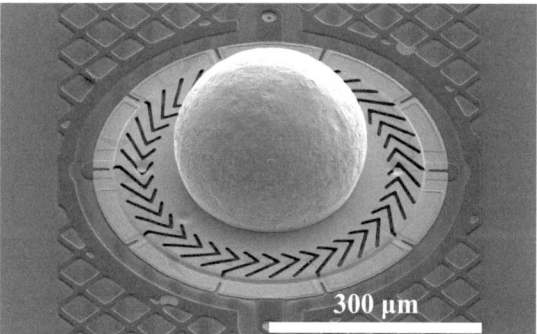

Figure 2.19: SEM picture of a single sensor. [1]

Fig. 2.20 shows a photograph of the released sensor array on a human finger. The picture demonstrates that a substrate with low intrinsic stress

35

could be achieved resulting in a device with little deformation in the released status, which is essential for integration. The individual sensing fibers are almost flat and parallel. However, all studies in this chapter are done on unreleased sensor arrays, before peeling them off from the fabrication carrier. The support allows for better reproducibility of measurement conditions and consequently better interpretation and comparison of the results.

Figure 2.20: Released sensor array with integrated capacitive sensors. Fibers are thin and flexible and show little warpage. [1]

2.4.3 Mechanical characterization & simulation comparison

The mechanical characterization of the taxels was studied in more detail at the beginning of the thesis and was presented in [1]. This section summarizes the measurements and a few additional studies. The tests lost of importance with the integration of the sensors in the soft silicone skin as introduced in chapter 3.

2.4.3.1 Measurement setup & devices

The sensors were characterized mechanically by measuring the force-displacement (FD) curves of the membranes with a Femto Tools FT-S1000. This tool uses a silicon MEMS structure to resolve forces with very high resolution and is ideal to quantify the spring characteristics of the membrane. Fig. 2.21 gives an overview of the tool and shows a microscope image of the probing (inset). A silicon needle with a 50 x 50 µm wide plateau at the end probes the sensors. The silicon probe needle is aligned manually to the sensors using a microscope, which works well in plane. Random errors occur from out of plane misalignment, which might result in contact slipping events.

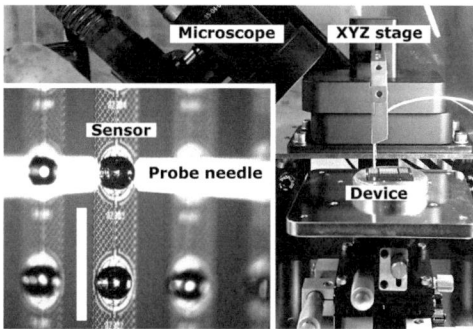

Figure 2.21: Femto tools setup with a FT-S1000 sensor for the measurement of FD curves. Overview on the general setup and microscope image of the probe needle in contact with a sensor (inset, scale bar 1 mm). [1]

Six chips from three different wafers were tested in this study, Table 2.12 gives an overview of the studies performed on each chip. Experiment 1 (repeatability) was performed to investigate random measurement errors. Experiments 2 - 4 were done to measure the membrane stiffness of membrane types M1 - M3 (see Fig. 2.3). On each sample, a calibration curve was generated by measuring a FD curve on the bare polyimide covered chip surface. This curve allows the estimation of the substrate and system (Femto Tools) compliance. The compliance is subtracted from the sensor curves and thereby allows the calculation of the actual spring constant of the membranes.

Table 2.12: Overview of the mechanical studies performed with the Femto tool, the arrays were introduced in Fig. 2.11. Adapted from [1].

Experiment type	Location	Repet. per sensor	n [#] sensors
1 - Repeatability	Array D1 - Sensor 1S1	12 or 3	1
2 - Stiffness M1	Array D1	1	9
3 - Stiffness M2	Array D2	1	4
4 - Stiffness M3	Array D3	1	4

2.4.3.2 Membrane simulation

Fig. 2.22 describes the simulation of the membrane behavior, introducing the boundary conditions and the mesh for membrane M3, M1 & M2 are simpler due to the simpler geometry. The membranes were simulated in Comsol and parametric geometry studies were performed with the LiveLink to Autodesk Inventor CAD. The membrane deformation in z direction is measured in the solder bump area for an applied force F_Z. Periodic boundary conditions reduce the complexity of the model (only $1/10$ of the membrane is simulated) and allow a fine mesh for accurate simulations. The mesh is mapped in z direction with five layers to accommodate the thin membrane behavior well. The two imperfections, which were assumed to modify the membrane behavior the strongest, are highlighted:

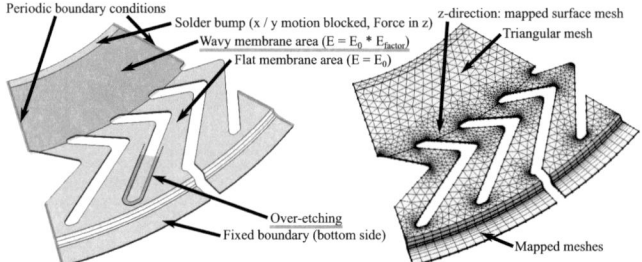

Figure 2.22: Overview on the simulation model for an M3 membrane with its boundary conditions (left) and the defined mesh (right). [1]

1. Over-etching: increases the width of all cut-outs in the membrane. This was quantified by microscopy analyses.

2. Wavy membrane area in the center: simplified by multiplying the E-modulus with a factor $E_{Factor} > 1$, hereby accommodating for the stiffness increase coming from structuring in z direction. This factor was estimated by approximating simulation results to the experimental results. The origin as well as actual measurement data of the wavy membrane area are displayed in Fig. 2.23.

Force sweeps between 100 - 400 µN allowed to extract the z deformation to calculate the membrane stiffness. Two cases were simulated as summarized in Table 2.13, the results are shown in Fig. 2.26.

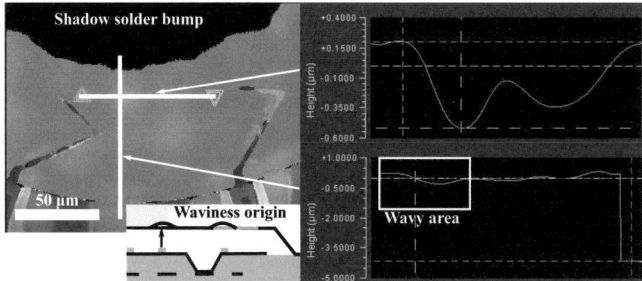

Figure 2.23: White light interferometer scan of a M2 membrane. The wavy area is shown in the line plots and the origin is highlighted in the sketch on the bottom. The waviness results from the limited planarization capability of the sacrificial layer over the stopper bumps. [1]

Table 2.13: Simulation parameters for the ideal and adapted membrane

Membrane type	Over-etching [µm]	E_{Factor}
Ideal	0	1
Adapted	2.5	6
Adapted value based on:	microscope measurement	parametric study

2.4.3.3 Results

FD plot analysis: Fig. 2.24 shows the FD plots of 9 sensors. The displacement range $h_{disp} = h_{membrane} - h_{stoppers}$ (see Fig. 2.2) is defined by the sacrificial layer process. Prior studies on bare silicon wafers showed process uniformities for the sacrificial layer of 3.3% WiW uniformity and 2.3 % WtW uniformity. Results may vary for the same process done on the device substrate, where surface topology of the subjacent layers as well as different exposed materials will influence the final layer thickness on a microscopic and macroscopic basis.

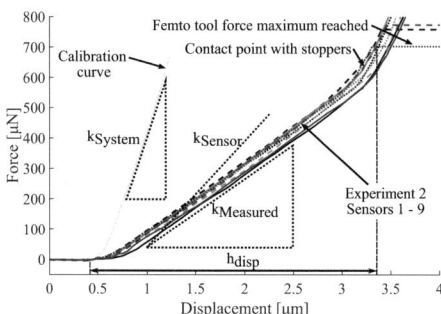

Figure 2.24: Measurement results (experiment 2, compare Table 2.12) from the Femto tool, describing the main characteristics for the analysis. [1]

The membranes show linear-elastic deformation over the whole displacement range. Two stiffness values k are extracted from the data:

1. $k_{Measured}$: Measured stiffness between 1 - 2.5 µm.

2. k_{System}: System stiffness (calibration curve, green).

The actual membrane stiffness k_{Sensor} is calculated based on the formula for two springs in series:

$$\frac{1}{k_{Sensor}} = \frac{1}{k_{Measured}} - \frac{1}{k_{System}} \tag{2.8}$$

Repeatability & Uniformity: Fig. 2.25a shows the measurement results for experiments 1 & 2. Experiment 1 (repeatability M1) shows the spread of random measurement errors on sensor 1 of each device. Experiment 2 (uniformity M1) displays the average and spread of the nine sensors measured in each case.

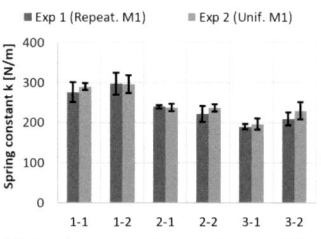 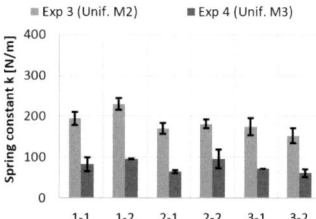

(a) Results of experiment 1 (repeatability M1) and 2 (uniformity M1).

(b) Results of experiment 3 (uniformity M2) and 4 (uniformity M3).

Figure 2.25: Mechanical experiments results for all devices with numbering 1-1 = "wafer number"-"device number". [1]

Table 2.14 displays that random measurement errors (Exp. 1) are in the same range as variations between sensors on the same substrate (Exp. 2). Random measurement error sources are expected to be:

1. Measurement uncertainties from the Femto Tool.

2. Slipping events in the probe needle - bumper contact.

Table 2.14: Statistical data of M1 membranes investigating repeatability and uniformity. Number of samples given in Table 2.12. [1]

Wafer-Device		1-1	1-2	2-1	2-2	3-1	3-2
Repeatability	% RSD	9.2	9.2	1.9	8.9	3.5	7.7
Uniformity	% RSD	3.0	7.3	3.8	3.7	7.0	9.5
Average Exp. 2	N/m	290.1	296.8	237.8	236.5	196.3	229.4

Actual differences from sensor to sensor may originate from processing variations. Little variations in sputtered metal thicknesses could be observed for the membrane process (sputtered film thickness variations: Ti 2.8%, Cu 1.7%, Au 2.5% RSD) as well as in the photolithographic processes defining the structures of the layers. The membrane multi-layer wet etch process however was done manually in a glass beaker and showed to be less repeatable, especially from wafer to wafer. Those problems can be tackled with appropriate equipment (e.g. spray etching), which was not available. Variations *within a device* are however expected to be strongly influenced by random errors. The very similar spread of experiments 1 & 2 supports this assumption. The averages *within wafers* (WiW) are a better index for actual processing variations. Wafers 1 & 2 showed good WiW uniformity, wafer 3 shows larger variation. A root cause could be the usage of the same etch

41

solution for all samples during fabrication, which resulted in significantly longer etch time on the third wafer.

Different membrane types and simulation comparison: Fig. 2.25b displays the results of experiments 3 & 4 (membrane variations) and Table 2.15 summarizes all statistical data. All membranes show similar WtW uniformity, confirming that those numbers are expected to result from processing variations which should have the same impact independent of the membrane type. The membrane type however influences the number of broken taxels. Membranes with a stiffness below 100 N/m proved to be more susceptible to collapse in the membrane release process.

Table 2.15: Overview of statistical data for different membrane types. Number of samples: M1 = 54 samples, M2/M3 = 24 samples. [1]

Membrane type		M1	M2	M3
Total average k	N/m	247.8	183.7	78.8
WtW uniformity	%	14.2	13.2	17.5
Sensors out of range	%	7.4	4.2	33.3

Fig. 2.26 puts the experimental data in perspective to the simulated membrane behavior. The data shows that the experimental data is not fully explainable by simulating the ideal membrane shape, which is mainly dependent on the area of the free membrane diameter and less on the spring structures (M2 & M3, when compared to M1, have almost similar stiffness). The simulations with adapted parameters (compare Table 2.13, same for all membranes) however allow a better description of the measured behavior.

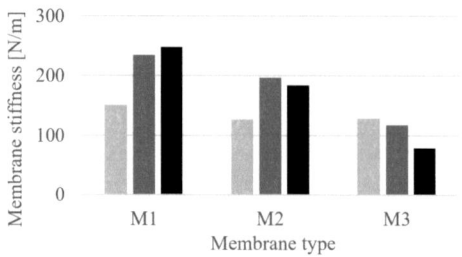

■ Sim. - ideal membrane ■ Sim. - adapted ■ Measurement

Figure 2.26: The measured membrane stiffness put into perspective to the simulation with ideal and adapted parameters, which were introduced in Table 2.13. [1]

2.4.3.4 Effect of the membrane thickness

GEN3 used membrane design M4 shown in Fig. 2.3, which is a slightly stiffer membrane. The variation of the membrane thickness proved to be the easiest method for further modifications of the stiffness as displayed in Fig. 2.27. Only the thickness of the sandwiched Cu layer was increased for this, while the Ti and Au layers were kept the same. The values at 1 μm are comparable to the data presented in Fig. 2.26. Each datapoint corresponds to one sensing array with 144 measured sensors. The sensor arrays were automatically measured with the characterization setup explained in chapter 5. This tool has a lower measurement resolution and therefore larger errors than the Femto Tools setup used in the previous studies, the automatic measurement however allowed the very fast acquisition of large amounts of data.

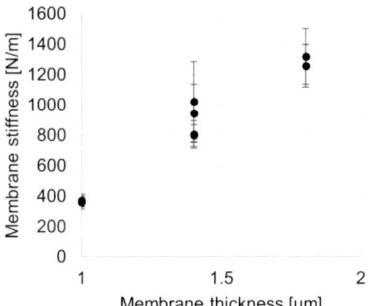

Figure 2.27: M4 membrane stiffness in dependence of the membrane thickness. 8 arrays measured with 144 taxels each.

2.4.4 Electromechanical characterization

The electromechanical characterization of the sensors is one of its key aspects, as the transduction of a mechanical pressure/force towards an electrically interpretable signal is the core function of the sensor itself. The measurement capabilities are also closely related to the readout electronics. In the course of this project four stages of readout electronics were developed (section 5.3). This section only summarizes some core concepts of the sensor behavior. The readout specifications and analysis of different failure modes are explained in sections 5.3 & 5.4, as a closer understanding of the electronics is important.

2.4.4.1 Measurement setup

Chapter 5 describes the measurement setup, which was used for electrome-chanical characterizations through all stages of the thesis. Fig. 2.28 depicts the general principle of measurement: an aluminum needle is attached to a force probe to manipulate the taxel. This needle is coated with a 5 µm thick parylene layer to avoid interference with the electrical measurements.

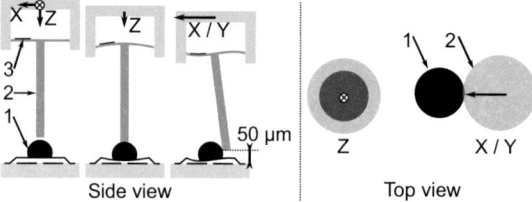

Figure 2.28: Manipulation of the taxel with the force probe (not to scale). 1) Taxel, 2) probe needle and, 3) strain gauge in the force probe. Adapted from [47].

2.4.4.2 General behavior

The setup is used to measure force-displacement-capacitance (FDC) curves as shown in Fig. 2.30. The force probe measures the applied force (black) while it drives down in z-direction. As for the Femto tool, the overall mea-sured compliance is on one side dependent on deformations in the measured membrane and on the other side on deformations in the measurement system as discussed in more detail in section 5.2.1. The range of applied force in this study is bigger (0-30 mN) than the range for the mechanical studies in the previous section (0-0.8 mN), which is marked as a blue box in the graph.

The capacitance change ΔC (red) is measured simultaneous to applying the force on the sensor. The measurement shows two distinctive regions:

1. Region 1 (R1): the membrane is deformed and small applied forces result in large changes of capacitance.

2. Region 2 (R2): the stopper structures are deformed and result in a range with decreased sensitivity but a larger measurable force range.

To confirm the plausibility of the measured data the actual membrane posi-tion (blue) is calculated with

$$z_{memb} = \frac{\epsilon A z_0}{\epsilon A + z_0 dC} \qquad (2.9)$$

where $A = \pi/4 * d^2_{electrode}$ is the electrode area and $z_0 = h_{membrane}$ is the initial distance of the membrane (Compare Fig. 2.29). It can be seen that the membrane position approaches 1 µm which is the designed height of the stoppers $h_{stoppers}$, confirming that no obstacles or residues reduce the deformation range.

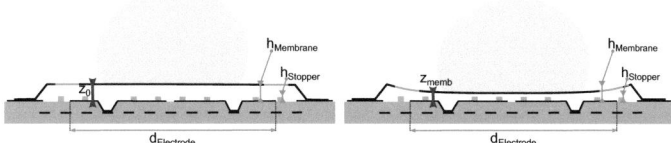

Figure 2.29: Sensor deformation and the important dimensions for the capacitance change. Further details were shown in Fig. 2.2.

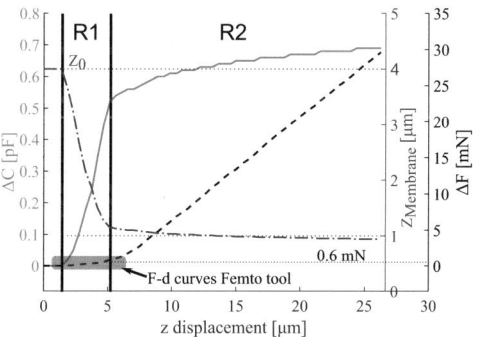

Figure 2.30: FDC curve taken with the setup. The applied force (black) and the capacitance (red) are measured. This capacitance is converted into the real sensor deformation (blue). [1]

As the measured displacement corresponds more to external deformations and is in most cases not relevant, the common representation was as a force - capacitance (FC) curve as shown in Fig. 2.31. The high (R1) and low sensitivity (R2) regions are better distinguishable in this representation.

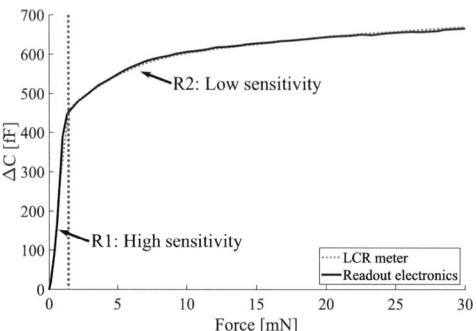

Figure 2.31: A Force-capacitance curve measured with the LCR meter (EV0) and the readout electronics (EV1) on the same taxel (different taxel than Fig. 2.30). [47]

2.4.4.3 Sensitivity

In [1] we used the same sensing arrays as previously described for the mechanical analysis for an electromechanical characterization. Fig. 2.32 presents the data of the M2 membranes taxels. Repeatability was investigated by measuring sensor 1S1 8 times under the same conditions.

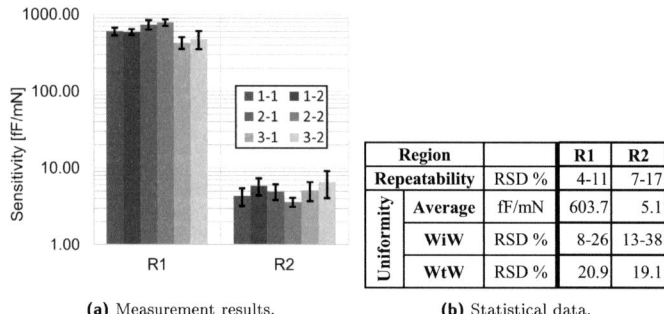

(a) Measurement results.   **(b)** Statistical data.

Figure 2.32: Sensitivities R1 & R2 of six devices with M2 sensors, total number of samples = 36. Adapted from [1].

The repeatability is worse than for the mechanical studies due to:

1. Measurement uncertainties: influenced by readout electronics and the relatively coarse step size in the z-movement.

2. Range definition: The sensitivity depends on the defined force range dF, especially in R1 where the transition point varies between sensors.

Additional variations originate from processing. In R1 the spread originates from membrane stiffness variations (see mechanical study, table 2.14) as well as the variations in the transition point. In R2 the contact deformations between the membrane and stoppers below is expected to influence the sensitivity.

2.4.4.4 Further studies

Over the course of the project several 10'000-100'000s of such measurements were performed due to the high automation degree of the characterization tool. The most important of those measurement series were:

- Statistical evaluation comparing several sensing arrays integrated in silicone skin presented in section 3.3.3.

- Endurance tests - compare sections 2.4.6 & 3.3.5.

- Temperature influence tests - compare section 2.4.7.

- Characterization of sensing arrays after the fabrication for the selection of good arrays for the finger fabrication.

2.4.5 3D sensing capabilities

This section describes the 3D sensing capabilities of the 3E sensors. The behavior was only studied qualitatively, as appropriate equipment for the precise alignment and manipulation of the sensors was not available.

Measurement setup Fig. 2.28 explains schematically the behavior of the force probe and sensor upon probe displacement in different directions, resulting in small deformations in the tactile sensor and larger deformations in the used force probe. The strain gauge in the force probe can only measure forces in Z direction (resulting in the characteristic plots displayed in Fig. 2.31), why probe displacements are plotted for all graphs.

The actual method of using a cylinder for the sideward actuation is not ideal, as slipping events between the two round bodies resulted in measurement disturbances and made it more difficult to precisely aim for the X and Y contact points (compare Fig. 2.28). The sideward actuations were performed with a 50 μm distance between the sensing array surface and the bottom of the probe needle.

Qualitiative results Fig. 2.33 shows the probe displacement - capacitance plots for the same sensor when actuated from different directions. It is visible that the three electrodes react differently when actuated from different directions. Forces in X and Y direction result in a tilting of the membrane, and the electrode opposed to the force application point shows the largest signal. All measurements show R1 & R2 as described further above.

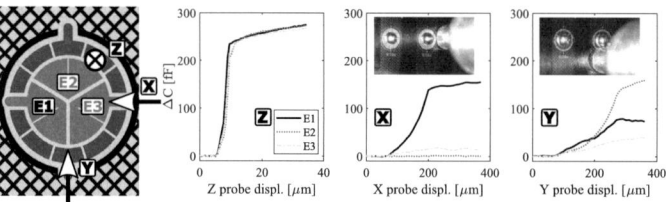

Figure 2.33: Measurement response of a 3E taxel upon actuation from different sides. [47]

3D force estimation The X, Y and Z components of the force acting on a 3E sensor were calculated based on a theoretical assumption due to a lacking, more precise, characterization. Fig. 2.34 shows the three electrodes of a 3E sensor in an X/Y coordinate system. The amplitude in Z direction and the X/Y components are calculated as follows, with E1 - E3 being the electrode capacitances in fF:

$$\begin{bmatrix} X \\ Y \\ Z \end{bmatrix} = \begin{bmatrix} -\sqrt{3}/2 & 0 & \sqrt{3}/2 \\ -0.5 & 1 & 0.5 \\ 1 & 1 & 1 \end{bmatrix} \cdot \begin{bmatrix} E1 \\ E2 \\ E3 \end{bmatrix} \tag{2.10}$$

The values for X & Y correspond to the lengths of the unit vectors (in white in Fig. 2.34) on the X/Y plane, with $\cos(30°) = \sqrt{3/2}$ and $\sin(30°) = 1/2$.

This conversion was used to evaluate the 3D forces acting on taxels after the integration into the artificial finger as presented in section 4.5.

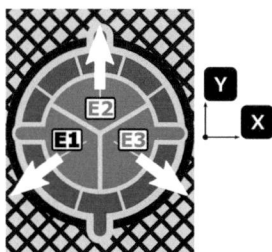

Figure 2.34: Schematic of the three electrodes in a taxel compared to the sensor X/Y coordinate system. [2]

2.4.6 Cycling stability & sensor overload behavior

Two cycling stability studies were performed on the taxels, in which the probe needle moved down from a non-contact state until an allowed maximum force was reached for 10'000 iterations:

1. Uncoated taxel: data presented in Fig. 2.35. This data replaces the originally published measurements in [1], which were measured with the LCR meter (EV0, compare section 5.3). The new electronics EV2 allowed a more stable measurement, which simplifies the data interpretation.

2. Silicone coated taxels: presented and discussed later in Fig. 3.9.

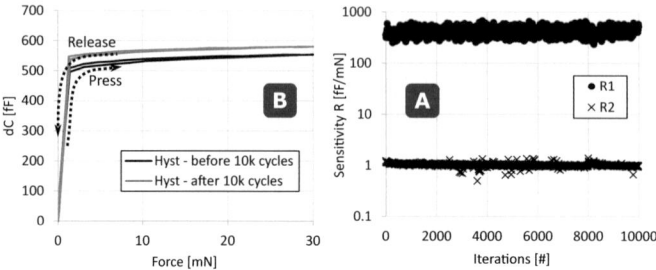

Figure 2.35: Taxel endurance test results over 10k iterations. A: Hysteresis of the taxel measurement before and after the test. B: Sensitivities R1 & R2 during the test.

Fig. 2.35 allows the following observations:

- The uncoated taxels show no significant hysteresis before and after the cycle test.

- Sensitivities R1 & R2 are clearly distinguishable and remain stable over 10k compressions. R2 has a slight run-in period and is generally stiffer for newer sensors.

- R1 has a larger measurement fluctuation as the amount of measurement points in the small deformation range is little and measurement inaccuracies from the force probe are more significant.

Overload behavior   A similar experiment at 80 mN studied the sensor overload behavior. Fig. 2.36 shows the compression and release behavior of the sensors before and after 50 actuations and the two degradation mechanisms of the sensors under high load. Both failure modes could be observed in previous tests on other sensors:

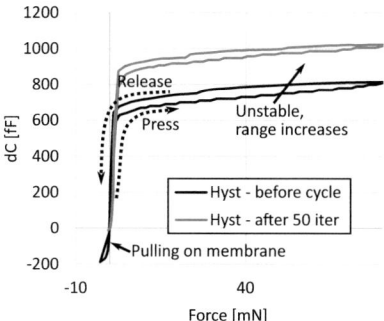

Figure 2.36: Compression and release of the sensors in the overload test. Data measured with EV0, replotted from [1].

1. Flattening of the solder ball by the probe needle, resulting in sticking between the sensor and the needle upon retraction. This is observable as a negative force in the first cycle. The $\Delta C = -188\,\text{fF}$ translates into an electrode distance of 38 μm (sensor pulled away from the electrodes), which is much larger than the designed compression range for the z actuation, resulting in membrane strain.

2. Increased maximum capacitance over the test duration, which is explained with micro molding of the solder ball onto the stopper structures (the membrane itself has limited structural integrity), resulting in a reduced gap size. This will ultimately result in either a sticking of the membrane on the bumpers or shortcuts with the subjacent electrode.

Possible improvements   The two failure mechanisms described are both related to the InSn solder bump, rather than to a membrane or stopper bump degradation. The used solder has a melting point of 118°C and is relatively soft at room temperature. The low melting point facilitated process integration, the actual process would however allow the integration of solders up to a melting point of 200°C. Both degradation mechanisms should be improved with such a change.

2.4.7 Characterization of temperature influence

Another study investigated the temperature dependency of the sensing performance; Fig. 2.37 displays the results. A Peltier element was clamped below the device and controlled the applied temperature with a PT1000 sensor and a Keithley 2510 TEC SourceMeter in a PID control loop. The data allowed a few important observations:

- A trend towards higher sensitivity is observable for higher temperatures (inset Fig. 2.37) in R1. The effect was not studied in further detail, there are however two potential root causes. Firstly, some membrane softening is expectable with a reduced Young's modulus at higher temperatures, the effect should however be rather small for metals in this temperature regime. Secondly, a CTE mismatch between the substrate (Si, PI2611 $\approx 3 \cdot 10^{-6} K^{-1}$, see Table B.1) and the membrane (Ti/Cu $9-16 \cdot 10^{-6} K^{-1}$) results in an additional expansion of the membrane, which could lead to slight buckling or to a reduction of intrinsic layer stress. This modification of membrane tension could result in an additional softening effect. Further, the force probe heated up when it got in contact with the taxels (through the heat-conducting Al probe needle). The probe is temperature compensated up to $50°C$. Higher temperatures resulted in slight drifts and influenced the measurement.

- The capacitive range increases for higher temperatures, especially above $60°C$. This effect however is reversible, which could be proven with another measurement at room temperature after the temperature cycle and no long term degradation is observable as in the overload tests. The effect can again be explained with a mismatch in CTE's of the substrate and membrane. The stronger expanding metallic membrane could therefore slightly buckle up, resulting in a larger $h_{membrane}$ and hereby a larger capacitive range.

- At $80°C$ sticking between the solder bump and probe needle gets an issue due to the solder melting point of $118°C$. A solder material with higher melting point should help to increase the possible temperature range.

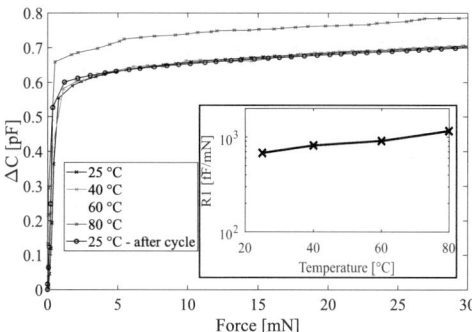

Figure 2.37: Results of the temperature characterization. Inset: sensitivity R1 calculated from two measurements at each temperature. Adapted from [1].

2.5 Manufacturing costs

The sensing technology itself is considered to be the largest cost factor for an artificial sensing skin. The fabrication costs for the sensing units were therefore estimated together with Vibuja Manichelvan in the course of her BSc thesis [63]. Details of the analysis can be found in her thesis, the most important results are summarized here.

The cost estimation was done in reasonable detail and included real pricing information about materials and capital equipment. They were estimated for a fabrication line of 200 mm wafers in Switzerland with Swiss wages, production hall costs and insurances. The size of the plant was tried to be estimated by floor plans and costs estimated based on necessary cleanroom areas. The case study was conducted with three scales. Table 2.16 shows the estimated production cost per fabricated wafer split into capital expenditures (CAPEX) and operational expenditures (OPEX). It also displays the total initial investment (total CAPEX) necessary to set up the production. Fig. 2.38 depicts the differences of the cost factors for the small and large scale fabrication.

Table 2.16: Wafer costs and total CAPEX for different fabrication volumes. Adapted from [63].

		Small scale	Medium scale	Large scale
Volume	wafer/year	1000	10'000	100'000
Devices	devices/year	10-20k	100-200k	1000-2000k
CAPEX	CHF/wafer	492	137	78
OPEX	CHF/wafer	522	236	169
Total Cost	CHF/wafer	1'014	373	247
Total CAPEX	CHF	6'341'473	17'161'049	99'377'460

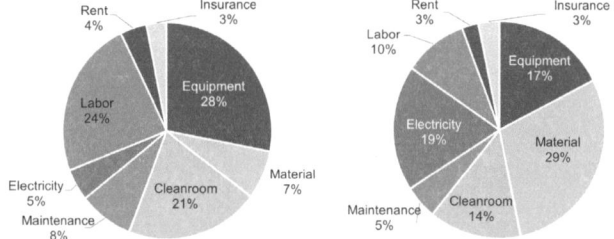

(a) Small scale production   **(b)** Large scale production

Figure 2.38: The cost breakdown into the cost factors for different fabrication volumes. Adapted from [63].

A few important conclusions were:

- Final device costs: One wafer can hold 10 - 20 sensing arrays, depending on the final array size. The actual price per device therefore has to be divided by this factor 10 - 20.

- Economies of scale: the effect is clearly visible for the gathered data. Small volume productions of the technology are expensive, why a fabrication partner makes sense. Some equipment in the small scale scenario for example cannot be used at full capacity.

- Cost reduction: Costs could be significantly cut by building up the fabrication line abroad. Additionally, it would need to be reconsidered if equipment from the semiconductor industry can be replaced by equipment designed for the flexible substrate / PCB industry. Agreeable

defect densities will depend on the final device design, which defines
the necessary process equipment and cleanroom levels.

2.6 Comparison of the unpackaged sensor technology

Table 2.17 puts the characteristics of the developed taxels in perspective to
other sensing skins. Some assumptions and conversions were necessary to
allow direct comparison of values. Forces are converted to pressures using
the unit cell size (sensor grid size in square) of the presented sensors. This
method results in a possible distortion by the fabricated grid sizes in different publications, was however unavoidable due to the different definitions
used. The actual contact area of the unpackaged taxel is very small, this
allows however the comparison of a uniformly applied pressure to a skin with
arbitrary size. The sensitivity can be divided by its nominal electrical value
to allow the comparison of different measurement principles:

$$S_P = \frac{d(\Delta C/C_0)}{dp} \; [kPa^{-1}] \qquad (2.11)$$

respectively

$$S_F = \frac{d(\Delta C/C_0)}{\Delta F} \; [N^{-1}] \qquad (2.12)$$

with $C_0 = C_{rerouting} + C_{sensor,0}$ being the nominal capacitance (section 2.1.5)
of the wiring in the substrate as well as the sensor and $dp = \Delta F/A_{sensor}$
being the applied pressure. The sensitivities of the two ranges are calculated
and displayed in Table 2.17.

The sensor presented in this work has high sensitivity and a small sensor unit
size compared to previous work. Those advantages are achieved with the very
compact sensor design as well as the small gap size between the membrane
and lower electrodes, which can be produced in a stable condition. The thin
and flexible membrane further results in very high sensitivities. Pressure
sensors coupled with OFET's as presented by Zhu et al. [33] can achieve
high sensitivities due to the direct pre-amplification, high gate voltages are
however needed to achieve higher sensitivities. Tested pressure ranges are
larger for larger sensors presented in other papers. The uncoated taxels
are tested up to 80 mN, a recommended range is however 30 mN (Table
2.17, column *Range*). The number of sensors presented in this work is in

Table 2.17: Overview on the achievements in perspective to other sensing skins. The sensor sensitivities and measurement ranges are given for the uncoated taxels introduced in this chapter as well as for taxels coated with 220 & 660 μm of silicone. The measured values are introduced later in section 3.3.3. Adapted from [1].

	Meas. Princ.	Grid size	Amount sensors	Range	S_P	S_F	Original information
Unit		μm	#	kPa	kPa^{-1}	N^{-1}	
This work, no coating				0.1 - 0.6	2.6e+0	2.6e+3	600 fF/mN 0.1-0.6 mN
				5 - 25	2.2e-2	2.2e+1	5 fF/mN 5 - 25 mN
This work, 220 μm coating	Cap	1000 (Sensor 500)	144	1 - 15	1.2e-1	1.2e+2	30 fF/mN 1 - 15 mN
				30 - 85	1.7e-2	1.7e+1	4 fF/mN 30 - 85 mN
This work, 660 μm coating				1 - 50	3.8e-2	3.8e+1	9 fF/mN 1 - 50 mN
				75 - 85	1.0e-2	1.0e+1	2.5 fF/mN 75 - 85 mN
Boutry et al [9]	Cap	~1500	81	0 - 1	1.9e-1	8.4e+1	0.19 kPa^{-1}
				10 - 20	4.0e-2	1.7e+1	0.04 kPa^{-1}
Lee et al [29]	Cap	2000	64	0 - 2.5	1.2e-1	3.0e+1	3% / mN 0 - 10 mN
Liang et al [30]	Cap	4000	16	0 - 30	1.0e-2	6.7e-1	67.2 %/N 0 - 0.5 N
				30 - 250	1.2e-3	7.7e-2	7.7%/N 0.5 - 4 N
Zhu et al. [33]	Cap + OFET	7500 (Sensor ~1600)	64	0 - 5	2.3e-1	9.2e+1	0.23 kPa^{-1} @V$_{GS}$ = 6V
Chun et al [31]	Res	1000	400	0.1 - 6	1.6e+0	1.6e+3	1.6 kPa^{-1}
				6 - 100	4.0e-2	4.0e+1	0.04 kPa^{-1}
Kim et al [42]	Res	1000	1024	0 - 600	2.0e-5	2.0e-2	2%/N 0 - 0.6N
				600 - 1000	1.0e-5	1.0e-2	1%/N 0.6 - 1 N
Kwon et al [43]	Res	2500	16	0			70 mV/N
Someya et al. [32]	Res + OFET	2540	256	N/A	N/A	N/A	

the midfield, a larger number of sensors however is possible. Most of the presented technologies will allow upscaling of the sensor arrays regarding the total number of sensors, ultimately limiting will be the connected readout electronics.

3 Sensor packaging in soft material

The packaging of sensors is an important factor for its characteristics and robustness to external influences. Large parts of this chapter were introduced in [2].

Silicone spray coating was chosen as the sensor packaging process due to its capabilities of covering the fragile MEMS by sequentially building up a sturdy, self-stabilizing layer. Additional advantages were the conformal coating capability of 3D objects as well as good average thickness control. The skin was sprayed with a mix of silicone diluted with n-Hexane to sufficiently reduce the viscosity. Nusil MED-4905 (see material table B.1) was used due to its resilience to brittle fracture and less drift with ageing when compared to more widely used materials like Sylgard 184. [64,65]

3.1 Related work in silicone spray coating

The spray technology in this work was developed based on inputs from Dr. Fergal Coulter, who uses it for the coating of 3D objects [66]. The process however needed significant adaption to allow the coating of fragile MEMS structures. Spray coating was previously explored to spray thin films of Sylgard 184 [67] with an airbrush pistol and 200 Fluid 20 cSt as a solvent. Further, it was used to spray multi-layer dielectric elastomer actuators [68]. The direct application onto flexible and fragile MEMS was not reported to the best of our knowledge.

3.2 Spray coating setup & material

Fig. 3.1 shows the semi-automated spray coating tool with its main components:

1. XYZ table, which was sourced from a commercial 3D printer including the control unit, which is interfaced with G-code.

2. The spray stage, which was the reconfigured and thermally isolated printing stage of the 3D printer.

3. Spray valve with two input ports for the air and material flow.

4. Two analog valves to control the flows.

The valves were controlled with an Arduino, which was interfaced with the control software. The control software and the user interface were programmed in Python and converted to an executable for an easy control of the spray process. For an auto-spray loop the user needs to define the process parameters as well as the outer dimensions of the area to be sprayed. The spray stage then covers this area with a meander-like pattern for a uniform coverage of the sprayed sample.

Nusil MED-4905 silicone was diluted with n-Hexane in a 1:4 ratio to achieve a low-viscosity fluid, which allows spraying. The samples were fixed on the spray stage with Kapton tape and the spray stage heated to 60°C during the spray process to cure the silicone during spraying.

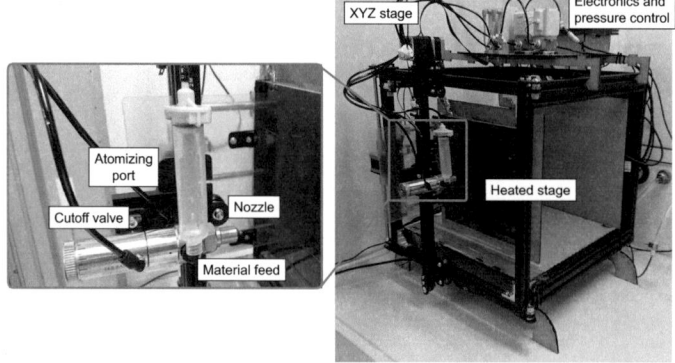

Figure 3.1: Spray coater used for the fabrication of the silicone skins with all its major components. [2]

3.3 Results

This section summarizes a few important studies on the process itself as well as the characterization of the embedded sensors in the silicone skin.

The sensor arrays were left on the silicon chip for all studies in this chapter and measured with the characterization setup shown in Fig. 5.1. The static and dynamic sensing characteristics were measured, and the endurance of the sensors in the skin tested. Some results presented in this chapter were measured by Felix Mähr in the course of his BSc thesis.

3.3.1 Process characterization

3.3.1.1 Standard processes

Process testing was performed on pristine Si wafer pieces. Some areas were masked with Kapton tape, followed by spraying the chip with the silicone layer. The Kapton tape was removed, the Si chips coated with a 10 nm Au layer in a sputter coater and the sprayed layer thicknesses measured with white light interferometry (WLI).

Two standard processes were elaborated, a fast and a slow spray coating process. Goal of the comparison was to understand if the application speed influences the curing and film properties. The spray speed was mainly adapted with the spray needle diameter. Table 3.1 summarizes the characteristics of the two processes, which achieved closed and conformal layers down to 5±0.5 µm thickness (thinner coatings are possible with process adaptions). All processes are scanned sprays with a meander shaped pattern. The spray area is selected significantly larger than the sample to get a uniform surface coating.

Table 3.1: Spray processes and their most important characteristics (Sample size per case: 4). The thickness of the coating is controlled with the volume of the used material.

Process	Spray time	RSD thickness	Av. thickness measured samples
	min / 100 µm	%	µm
Slow	90.5	10.9	4.8
Fast	3.5	4.5	53.0

The slow spray process was initially used to understand better the coating behavior of the sensors. It was however completely replaced by the fast spray coating process towards the end of the thesis, as no advantages for the slow coating could be observed when final thicknesses of 200 µm or more are desired. This might not be valid for applications where a thinner coating is desirable.

3.3.1.2 Curing

Samples were pre-cured on the spray stage through the heated plate but also placed in a convection oven for >2 hours of post-curing. This process was tested at 60 - 100 $°C$. The manufacturer recommends a curing of 5 min at 150 $°C$, which was not tested due to the incompatibility with the solder material (118 $°C$ melting point). No obvious differences were observed on the films, the mechanical parameters were however not tested in detail. The curing temperature however influenced the sensor behavior as described later in section 3.3.3.

3.3.1.3 Defects

Fig. 3.2 shows a microscope image of a sensing array with a 660 µm thick silicone layer. The conformity of the coating over each taxel can be seen, but also some defects, which result from larger dust particles acting as nucleation sources in the spray process. Those clots change the characteristics of the sensors below and should be avoided to have a repeatable sensor response.

These defects resulted from sample handling and from particles in the air flow during spraying. The defect density for slowly spray coated samples was higher due to longer spraying times. The behavior was improved by periodic cleaning of the used fume hood. Shifting the process to a cleanroom would however be advisable.

Figure 3.2: Sensing array after spray-coating 660 μm of silicone. 45° angle view.

3.3.2 Optical appearance & coating conformity

The optical appearance of the spray coated layer depends on the thickness. Thin coatings (<20 μm) have a rough appearance while thicker coatings have a smooth finish. This effect is expected to result from the decreasing significance of the single, incoming droplets. Fig. 3.3 shows microscope images of taxels with different coating thicknesses. Thin layers are optically difficult to analyze due to their higher surface roughness, while thicker layers get translucent and more reflective again.

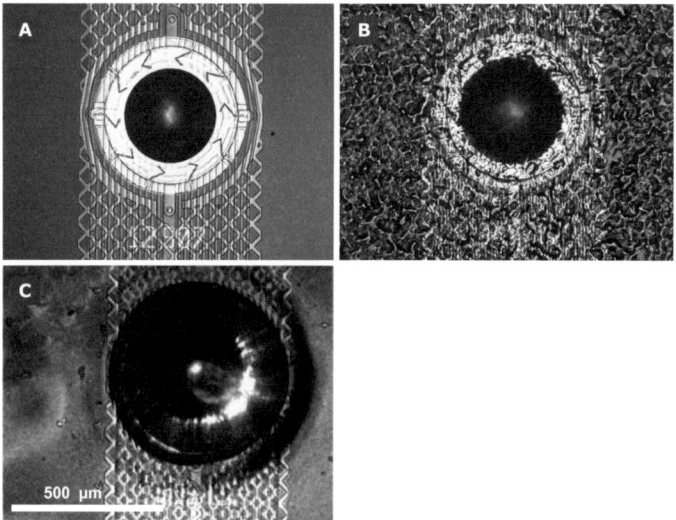

Figure 3.3: Sensors with different coating thickness. A) No coating, B) 5 µm coating, C) 100 µm coating.

Coating conformity The conformity of the silicone coating over the sensors was measured with white light interferometry after gold-coating the samples. The height of the bumper relative to the area between the sensors was measured for different silicone thicknesses, and is displayed in Fig. 3.4. The measurement was rather unreliable for thinner silicone thicknesses due to the larger roughness, and more reliable for silicone thicknesses >100 µm. This data was used to optimize the sensor model described later in section 4.2. The relation between h_{bump} and h_{skin} was linearly approximated. Other approximations of the relationship resulted in little variations of the simulation results, why the experimental data was decided to be sufficient.

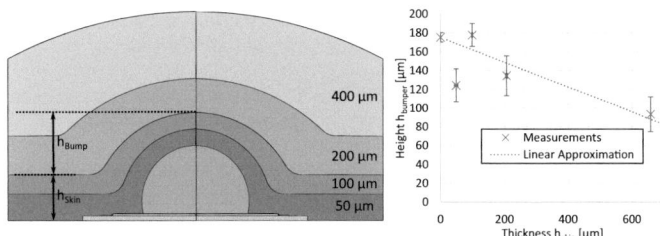

Figure 3.4: Model of the taxel with coating. The coating is only partially conformal and was measured for different coating thicknesses (horizontal
error bars too small to be visible). Sample size: 7 per thickness.
Only DR arrays were used and the conformity measured in vertical
direction, where taxels have a 2 mm gap distance. Measured taxels were distributed over the array and selected based on the signal
strength in the WLI after the Au coating (very weak signal).

3.3.3 Embedded sensors - Static characterization

The goal of this study was the investigation of the static sensing characteristics for different silicone skin thicknesses.

3.3.3.1 Experimental

Table 3.2 shows the process conditions for the tested six sensing arrays (3x
DL, 3x DR) from three chips.

Table 3.2: Process conditions for sensor coating. Sample colors correspond to
the data in 3.6.

Arrays	Spray time [min/100 μm]	Cure temp. [°C]
Chip 1 DL Chip 2 DR	90.5	80
Chip 2 DL Chip 1 DR	3.5	
Chip 3 DL Chip 3 DR		60

All taxels were used for the statistical evaluation except obviously faulty taxels, which could be grouped in three main sources of errors:

1. initially broken supply/readout lines in the flexible substrate (compare section 5.4).

2. unreliable contact with the probe card due to misaligned or contaminated pads (compare section 5.4). This behavior can theoretically be improved by multiple attempts of contact pad alignment, the used probe needle array however was not in a good condition anymore.

3. clots of silicone on the chip which resulted from larger dust particles described (compare section 3.3.1.3).

3E taxels on DR sensing arrays were discarded from the statistical analysis as they cannot be directly compared with 1E taxels.

3.3.3.2 Results

Fig. 3.5A displays that taxels maintain their high (R1) and low (R2) sensitivity regions after coating. Fig. 3.5B shows the averaged curves of chip 3 (1x DL, 1x DR) of all working taxels for an increasing skin thickness. The amount of measurable taxels fluctuated strongly as visible in Table 3.3, especially due to the unreliable contact of the probe card. The averaging of all curves results in the artifact of a more rounded transition between R1 & R2. The regions get less distinguishable for thicker coatings for two reasons:

1. the optical alignment of the force probe needle and taxels gets more difficult, and the misalignment results in an initially lower sensitivity upon contact.

2. the coating thickness uniformity and included smaller dust particles partially shifted the characteristics of some taxels, which still were considered as valid.

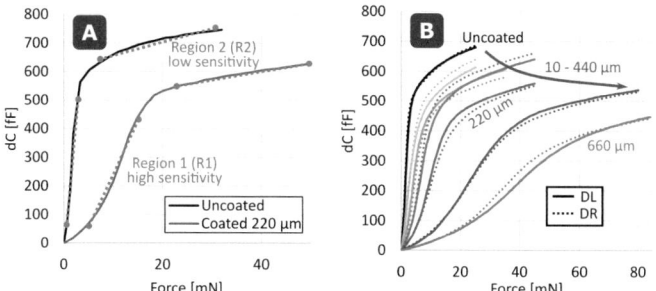

Figure 3.5: Static characterization of the taxel sensitivity with varying skin thickness h_{skin}: A: General behavior of uncoated and coated taxels. B: Averaged curves of all taxels for chip 3. [2]

Table 3.3: Thickness & measurable taxels in each iteration for chip 3. Complete missing rows or lines are related to misaligned contact pads. The behavior is similar for chips 1 & 2.

Thickness [µm]	0	10	71	126	237	454	661
Thickness Std [µm]		0.5	1.6	9.3	17.2	11.8	8.8
DL (max 144)	141	89	104	115	131	68	64
DR (max 36)	21	7	19	27	32	29	11

Fig. 3.6 show the extracted sensitivities R1 & R2, error bars are shown representatively for the two arrays of chip 3. No influence of the spraying speed or curing temperature could be observed. Fig. 3.6A depicts a relatively strong decline of R1, as the increasing skin thickness strongly influences the deformation of the thin metal membrane in the taxel. The decline for R2 is less prominent, as this region corresponds to small deformations in the polymer studs (see section 2.4.4.2), which are less dominated by deformations in the upper silicone layer.

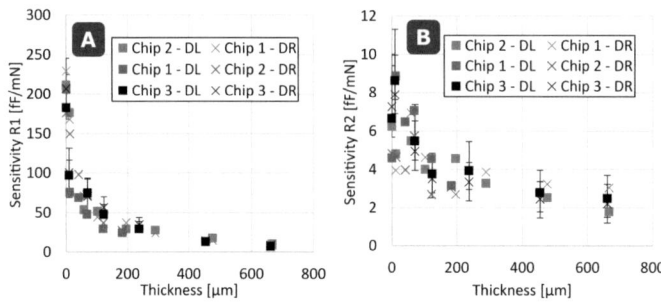

Figure 3.6: Static characterization of the taxel sensitivity with varying skin thickness h_{skin}: R1 & R2 for different thicknesses. [2]

Fig. 3.5B additionally shows a reduced capacitance range for a thicker skin, which was more prominent for higher curing temperatures (chip 1 & 2). The mismatch in thermal expansion coefficients (CTE's) of the coated silicone and subjacent taxels might result in slight compression of the taxels. Lower curing temperatures are possible but increase the necessary curing time. It is hypothesized that this effect is less prominent when integrated on a soft finger compared to this on-chip study, as shrinking around the taxels would be uniform rather than focused on only the top silicone layer.

3.3.4 Embedded sensors - Dynamic characterization

3.3.4.1 Experimental

The same sensing arrays were characterized after each iteration of silicone application (compare Table 3.3) for their dynamic sensing capabilities. Four 1E taxels per array (starting in location 1S1, choosing the first four responsive taxels) were excited between 1 - 600 Hz and three measurement iterations per taxel were performed.

The setup includes an Analog Discovery 2 (AD2) for the generation of a sinusoidal input wave, a piezo amplifier (Thorlabs BPC 301) and a piezo actuator (Thorlabs PAS005) with a metal needle having the same dimensions as for the static taxel characterization (0.5 mm diameter tip). The taxel to be measured is approached with the microscope video image, then the contact is detected by measuring the taxel directly. After this definition of the contact position, the piezo actuator drives down by a defined indentation depth to guarantee good mechanical contact of the probe needle and taxel during the whole vibration measurement. The piezo actuator is used to apply a sinusoidal mechanical vibration with the wave form generated by the AD2. The capacitance of the actuated taxel is converted to an actual membrane position with equation 2.9 resulting in Fig. 3.7A. Here a 1000 Hz vibration is applied to showcase how also higher frequencies can be easily measured and distinguished. The sinusoidal shape of the movement is clearly visible in the second graph. The displacement signal is analyzed with a Fast Fourier Transform (FFT) to extract the amplitude of the measured vibration at the mechanical excitation frequency, resulting in data as shown in Fig. 3.7B. The applied amplitude is well distinguishable over the noise level and can be extracted.

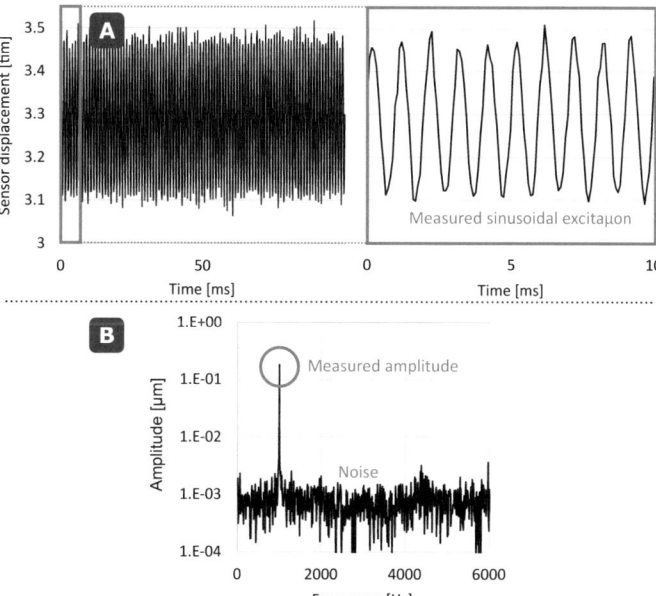

Figure 3.7: Raw data in the dynamic sensor characterizations. A: Displacement signal, B: FFT. Adapted from [2].

3.3.4.2 Results

Fig. 3.8A shows the measured amplitude A_{meas} versus the applied amplitude $A_{applied}$ for an increasing silicone thickness for the taxels of chip 1 - DR. The averages of the four taxels and three measurements each are displayed, and the error bars are given representatively for the first and last measured curve. The displayed characteristics were similar for the other three sensing arrays. The piezo actuator, its controller and the setup define the transmission curve for the uncoated taxel, as the taxel can completely follow the forced vibration. This assumption was verified with measurements in a laser doppler vibrometer (LDV):

- the transmission curve of the piezo actuator (without the setup, as integration was not possible) showed a similar decline of the measured amplitude for higher frequencies.

- The first eigenfrequency of the uncoated taxels was measured for 12 taxels to be in the range of 19.3 ± 2.9 kHz (dominated by the variation in mass of its solder bump) with a theoretical eigenfrequency of

$$f = \sqrt{\frac{k}{4\pi^2 m}} = 17.7 kHz \qquad (3.1)$$

with k being the membrane spring constant (compare Fig. 3.5 - uncoated taxels) and m being the mass of the solder ball (compare Fig. 2.2). Considering the large spectral range between the first eigenfrequency and the observed range of 1-600 Hz, a flat transmission curve is expected.

Some important observations from Fig. 3.8A are:

- The transmission of the vibration is damped by applying a thicker silicone layer, thus thicker silicone layers reduce the sensitivity.

- The transmission curve with a linear decline (decline originating from actuator transmission curve) observed for the uncoated taxels shifts towards a bent transmission curve for coated taxels with a maximum transmission at around 200 Hz. Lower frequencies are therefore damped slightly more, which is explained with the viscoelastic characteristics of the silicone.

- For higher frequencies (even for extended tests up to 1.5 kHz) the coated taxels showed no declines when compared to the uncoated taxels, the full necessary bandwidth of 0-500 Hz therefore can be well measured.

- The coated taxels have a higher RSD resulting from variations between taxels.

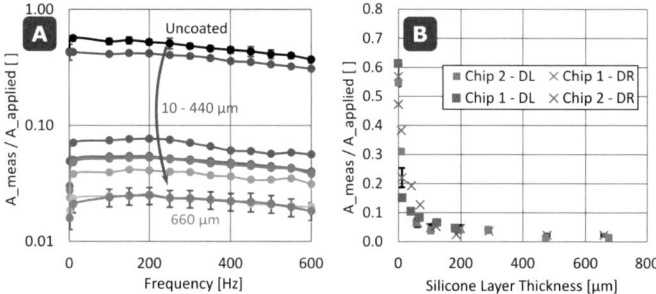

Figure 3.8: Dynamic characterization of the taxels, showing their transfer characteristics in dependence of frequency and silicone layer thickness. [2] A: color code as in Fig. 3.5, B: color code as in Fig. 3.6, same samples.

Fig. 3.8B shows the average of each transmission curve for the four measured sensing arrays versus the silicone layer thickness, the error bars are shown representatively for the curves of chip 1 - DR (data discussed in Fig. 3.8A). This data allows a few additional observations:

- The decrease in sensitivity for thicker silicone layers is similar as in the static experiments (Fig. 3.6A).

- No difference between faster or slower coating processes (red vs. blue data points) can be observed here as well.

3.3.5 Endurance tests

The coating endurance was tested by compressing two taxels (S1 & S2, sensors 1S1 & 1S2) with a 220 µm thick silicone coating with the force probe for 10'000 times up to 85 mN (maximum of the force probe). Fig. 3.9A shows R1 & R2 of the two taxels. Important observations are:

- No degradation can be observed for R1 over 10'000 cycles, R2 shows a short run-in period as previously discussed for uncoated taxels in section 2.4.6, where this behavior was explained with the initially plastic deformation of the polymer studs below the membrane.

- R1 shows lower noise than in Fig. 2.35, as the force range is larger, decreasing the effect of force probe measurement uncertainties.

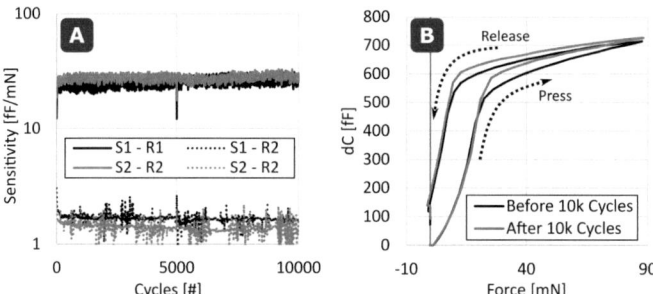

Figure 3.9: Endurance test for two taxels with a 220 µm thick skin, as well as the taxel hysteresis before and after the test.

Additionally, the hysteresis of the taxel was measured before and after the 10'000 cycles and is displayed in Fig. 3.9B with the following observations:

- The slight difference in R2 from before and after the cycling is observable.

- Taxels with a coating show a hysteresis, which is explained with the viscoelastic behavior of the silicone and was not observed previously for uncoated taxels (see section 2.4.6). It is expected that this hysteresis cannot be avoided for the soft material integration.

3.4 Summary

The silicone skin is an effective method to cover the taxels with a protective layer against mechanical damage or media exposure. The skin thickness h_{skin} influences the static and dynamic sensing capabilities of the sensors and a thicker skin reduces the sensitivity, which is expected. The data gathered in this chapter is further used to validate the simulation model in section 4.2 and allows the transfer of the sensitivity information from this on-chip data to a soft silicone fingertip. The sensitivity can be combined with the performance parameters of the readout electronics to calculate the force resolution presented in Table 5.5. 440 - 660 µm coatings are expected to be optimal for the human skin replication. The developed fast spray coating process (3.5 min / 100 µm) proved to be ideal for this application, and a curing at $60°C$ for 2h is reliable. Further optimizations of the spray speed are possible, were however not in the scope of this thesis.

The developed, semi-automated spray coater setup proved to be a reliable tool for the layer application. A full characterization of spray uniformities and repeatabilities is to be done, better probe analysis equipment however would be important. The measurement reliability of the used WLI was not good for highly translucent and rough layers, asking for several repetitions in measurements due to low signal quality. Most processing issues arose from particle contaminations due to the unclean working environment of the spray coater setup. This resulted in the defects shown in Fig. 3.2 or also in a clogged spray nozzle due to particles in the sprayed solution. The latter was not critical for the process, but would need to be solved for a higher level of automation.

4 Artificial Fingertip

This chapter summarizes the work and results of building an artificial fingertip with the integrated sensing skin. While other applications are possible, this challenge was chosen in the course of the thesis.

First, the design of an artificial finger bulk is presented. Verified simulations then allow to transfer the taxel data from section 3.3.3 to the soft fingertip to analyze design parameters. Artificial fingertips are built and several studies are presented which show the sensing capabilities of this technology.

4.1 Artificial finger bulk

A human finger was measured as a reference and a simplified silicone body was designed to replicate the mechanics. The measurement of the human finger was part of the MSc thesis project of Lorenz Kehrbein. The sensor simulation data is based on results from the BSc thesis project of Andri Caviezel, which includes previous work of David Zürcher and Severin Siegrist.

4.1.1 Human finger measurement

A left index finger was taken as a reference and the softness of the finger was measured along the X & Y coordinates as displayed in Fig. 4.1a with the characterization setup shown in Fig. 5.1, using the 0.5 mm wide needle. Movie `https://youtu.be/Tf3dvwOXeoQ` shows a screen recording of the GUI at the characterization setup. The data is not statistically representative for an average human, but should give a rough design value for the stiffness of the artificial fingertip. Fig. 4.1b shows a typical FD curve measured on the finger. The measured data needs to be compensated by the calibrated tool compliance (see section 5.2.1), resulting in the compensated FD curve (in black).

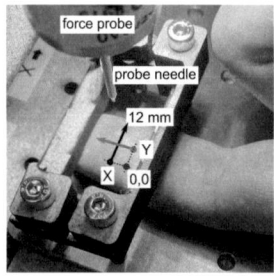
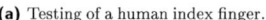

(a) Testing of a human index finger.

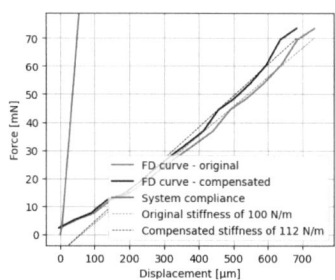

(b) FD curve on a human finger.

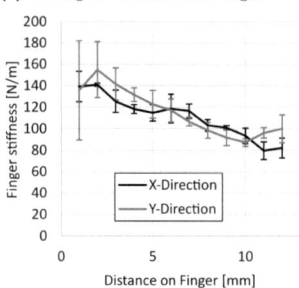

(c) Finger stiffness over different locations on the human finger. 4 measurement iterations in x direction, 3 in y direction.

Figure 4.1: Softness characterization of a human finger. [2]

Fig. 4.1c shows the measured stiffness between 10 - 70 mN along the X & Y direction of the index finger. The following observations can be made:

- The finger stiffness is not symmetric along the X or Y direction for the tested index finger, independent of a forward or reverse order of the measurements. The finger is stiffer towards the joint (Y direction) and on the outer side of the index finger (X direction). The assymmetry in X direction is expected due to the thicker skin on the outwards-facing side of the index finger. Other fingers might have a more symmetric profile, were however not tested.

- An average stiffness of 113 N/m in the force range of 10-70 mN could be measured for the indentation with the 0.5 mm wide cylindrical probe needle at the center of the finger. This was used as a rough target value for the artificial fingertip.

4.1.2 Design & Fabrication

A simplified finger was designed consisting of a 3D printed "bone" and a Dragonskin 20 silicone structure. The molding parts for the definition of the finger structure are 3D printed out of PLA, the finger bone, which remains in the model, is printed out of PETG (see Fig. 4.2a). The parts are screwed together after putting talcum powder on all removable mold parts to reduce sticking. Dragonskin 20 is mixed in a ratio 1:1, trapped air bubbles are removed in a vacuum desiccator and the mixture is poured into the mold, followed by another vacuum desiccator process to remove trapped bubbles. The fingers are cured for 4h and then taken out of the molds. Fig. 4.2b shows a photograph of such a fabricated finger.

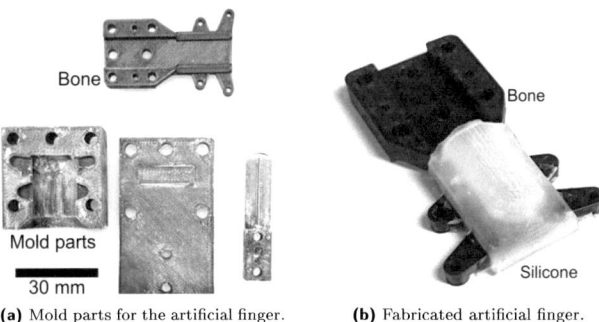

(a) Mold parts for the artificial finger.   **(b)** Fabricated artificial finger.

Figure 4.2: Overview fabrication artificial finger bulk.

4.1.3 Results

The very soft characteristics of the human finger could be achieved by a 1.4 mm thin silicone structure (crosscut in Fig. 4.3) with an air cavity, which is similar to the sturdy dermis and very soft finger pulp in a human finger [10]. The stiffness of the finger in the symmetry plane was evaluated by simulation (142 N/m, see next section 4.2.1 for the methods) and validated with four fabricated fingers (144 ± 11.5 N/m). Variations are explained by a ±0.1 mm positioning accuracy of the 3D printed molds.

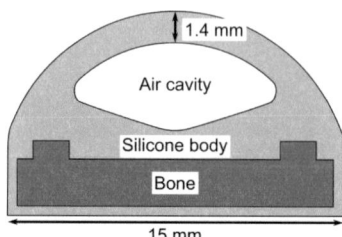

Figure 4.3: Crosscut drawing of the artificial finger used for the replication of the mechanics. [2]

The artificial finger is slightly stiffer than the human finger (113 N/m) as even thinner silicone structures were less reliable due to trapped air bubbles and the limited positioning accuracy of the 3D printed molds. The finger model however was validated as accurate by comparing with measurement data.

4.2 Simulation of sensing behavior and finger integration studies

This section presents the simulation results for the coated taxels on a chip and compares them with the previously presented data. The validated models are then used for design studies of the taxel integration into an artificial finger.

4.2.1 Simulation environment

Simulations were performed in COMSOL. All silicone materials were simulated as hyperelastic materials, the material parameters were approximated either with prior material tests in the characterization setup (Dragonskin 20 - Evaluated Young's modulus of 0.495 MPa) or fitted to experimental data (Nusil MED-4905 - 2.4 MPa). The taxel was simplified as a polyimide strip (8.5 GPa) and a closed metal membrane out of Ti (120 GPa, Cu is similar with 130 GPa). All material parameters are summarized in Table B.1.

Simulations were performed by indenting the model with a body in the shape of the aluminum needle used in the characterization setup (Fig. 4.4), the friction coefficient between the needle and the silicone was assumed to be 0.3. The needle indentation depth was plotted over the applied force for the evaluation of the finger stiffness. For the evaluation of the embedded taxel sensitivity the differential position between the upper and lower electrode in the taxels were extracted in relation to the applied force.

The simulations in this section were divided in two main cases executed on the same model as shown in Fig. 4.4:

1. *Taxel on chip*: the plane directly below the taxel and the surrounding silicone skin is fixed, corresponding to the measurements in the static characterization.

2. *Taxel on finger*: the fixed boundary condition is moved to the bottom of the simplified silicone finger structure that was validated in the previous section.

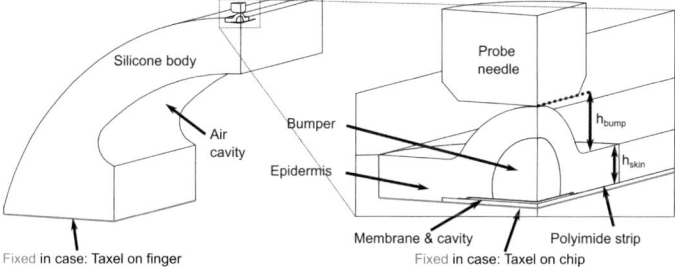

Figure 4.4: Simulation model for simulating the taxel response to different stimuli, either with a fixed plane directly below the taxel (right - *taxel on chip*) or at the bottom of the silicone finger (left - *taxel on finger*). [2]

The thickness of the silicone skin h_{skin} was varied to evaluate the taxel sensitivity. The coating conformity $h_{bump} = f(h_{skin})$ is discussed in section 3.3.2.

4.2.2 Results

Fig. 4.5 shows the simulation results of some relevant cases compared to the experimental data provided in 3.6A. The experimental data correlates to the curve *taxel on chip - 2.4 MPa*, this being the Young's modulus showing a good fit to the measured data. Two case studies were performed:

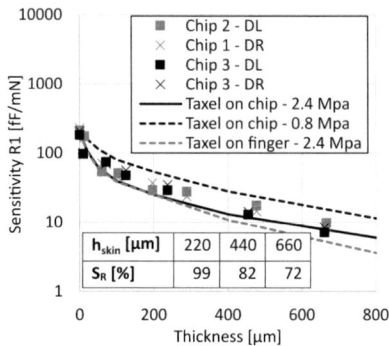

Figure 4.5: Measurement results compared to simulation data (*taxel on chip - 2.4MPa*) and exploration of the behavior upon implementation of the sensors on the soft finger. [2]

1. **Softer material**: the simulations showed that a reduction of the Young's modulus to $1/3$ (curve *taxel on chip - 0.8 MPa*) would result in a two times higher sensitivity for all thicknesses. Softer skins are therefore preferential, as a thicker skin can result in the same sensitivity.

2. **Sensor sensitivity on finger**: The most important comparison is made between the two cases *taxel on chip - 2.4 MPa* & *taxel on finger - 2.4 MPa*, the inset in Fig. 4.5 displays the sensitivity ratio

$$S_R = \frac{R1_{TaxelOnFinger}}{R1_{TaxelOnChip}} \tag{4.1}$$

for different silicone skin thicknesses. For a thin silicone skin the difference between the two cases is marginal while it gets more significant for thicker layers. This behavior is intuitive considering the ratio of the silicone thickness below and above the taxels. These results allow the transfer of the statistical information gathered for the taxels on chip to taxels on finger. Table 5.5 uses the extracted S_R and calculates the resulting force resolution, which is important for the skin layer design.

4.3 Fabrication of the integrated Fingertip

A sensing array is pre-selected (>90% working taxels) by measuring the taxel responses while the array is still fixed on the silicon carrier chip. Upon this,

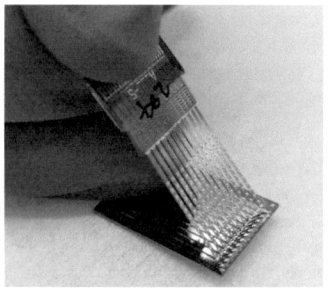

(a) Release of the sensing array

(b) Laser-cut stiffeners

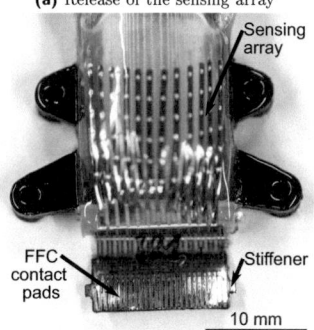

(c) Finger with attached sensing array and stiffener.

Figure 4.6: Fabrication steps for the artificial finger.

the silicon chip is cracked in the middle and the whole device is peeled off the silicon carrier as shown in Fig. 4.6a, leaving the thin flexible substrate with the taxels. This flexible substrate is too thin for the flexible flat cable (FFC) connector, why an additional stiffener part is necessary. This stiffener part is fabricated by sticking four layers of 80 µm thick Kapton tape onto each other and cutting the stiffener structure with a laser cutter. Fig. 4.6b displays those laser-cut stiffener structures, which are then taped to the back side of the FFC contact pad area (Fig. 4.6c).

The spray coater is prepared as explained in section 3.2 and the silicone mix is loaded. The fabricated finger is spray-coated with a thin layer of uncured silicone, making the surface sticky. The sensing array is then put on the finger and the sensing fibers arranged manually with tweezers to distribute them evenly on the finger surface. Upon this, the artificial finger with the attached sensing array is fixed on the spray coater stage again, and the silicone skin layer is sprayed in the same way as if a flat sensing array is covered with the silicone skin. The coating thickness depends on the curvature of the finger as the spraying was performed perpendicular to the finger. This behavior could be improved by an additional rotational axis in the spray coater setup, which was not implemented in the course of the thesis. After the curing of the finger, the contact pad array of the flexible substrate is clipped into the FFC connector of the small readout PCB and the readout PCB fixed with screws onto the measurement finger.

Fig. 4.7A shows the integrated finger from the front compared to a human reference finger. Fig. 4.7B shows the back side, featuring a downscaled version of the readout PCB (see section 5.3.3).

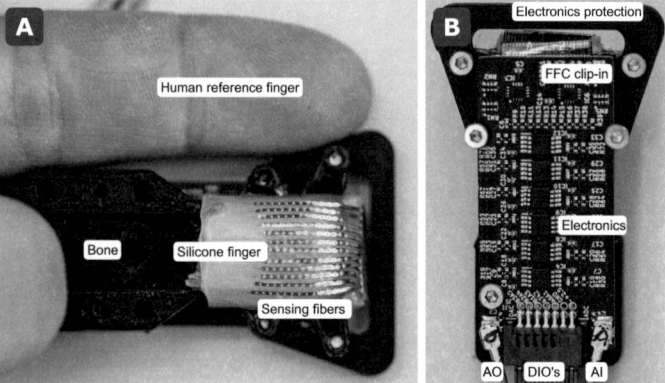

Figure 4.7: A) Artificial fingertip in comparison to the human reference fingertip. B) Backside with the miniaturized PCB for analog signal routing. [2]

Table 4.1 summarizes the artificial fingers described in more detail in this chapter, the full list of fabricated fingers can be found in Table A.4. Two versions of taxel embedding were tested (all devices are GEN3 with M4 membrane types - Fig. 2.3):

1. Standard: silicone covers the taxels and no silicone enters the cavity between membrane & electrode.

2. Stiffened: a controlled amount of silicone can enter through the membrane cut-outs, which stiffens the outer membrane region. This version was fabricated to analyze if the membrane is the source of signal

degradation (compare section 4.5.5 for details), has however several disadvantages summarized at the end of the chapter.

Table 4.1: Artificial fingers closer investigated in this chapter.

Finger	Coating thickness [µm]	Array type	Membrane type	Experiments
F14	200	DR	Standard	All initial experiments, feature extraction neural networks (section 4.6)
F24	600	DL	Standard	Data in [2]. Similar as F30, data for reference in Appendix C.2
F26	400	DL	Stiffened	Robustness study, surface classification
F30	400	DR	Standard	Robustness study

4.4 Results - single sensor characteristics

A first experiment studied the single taxel response on finger F14 (see Table 4.1) with the 0.5 mm wide probe needle pointing on one taxel. Fig. 4.8 shows a photograph and the resulting FC curve of this test, performed three times in a row on the taxel at the very top of the finger. Testing was only possible for the taxels at the top of the fingertip, as the probe needle tended to slip down the finger surface on the tilted periphery, making measurements impossible. The characteristic curve shows similar behavior as on the flat chip for small forces (R1 & R2, compare Fig. 3.5), the capacitance however starts to decrease at 40 mN again. This behavior is expected to originate from the local bending of the finger bulk under pressure, resulting in a bulging of the electrodes under the membrane. Earlier generations of the sensing fingers with a stiffer bulk did not show this behavior. This behavior is especially prominent for very pointy loads as for the case of this needle and plays less of a role for forces applied on a larger area, as local bending radii of the fibers are smaller.

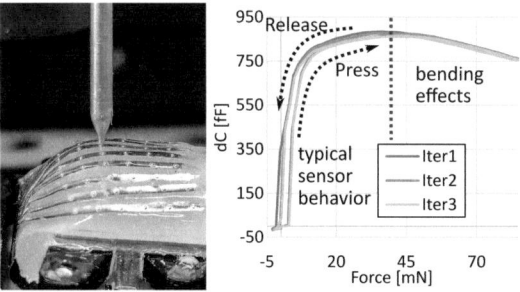

Figure 4.8: Single taxel characteristics after the integration on a soft finger. Left) photograph of the experiment, right) measurement data. [2]

Standard vs. stiffened membranes   Fig. 4.9 shows a comparison of nine logged sensors on F26 & F30 (400 µm skin, less sensitive) upon compression of the center taxel on the top of the artificial fingertip. Important conclusions are:

- Standard membranes are more sensitive and surrounding taxels show generally no response to stimuli. This however might depend on the location of the taxel on the finger and the manipulation. The initially small response relates to taxel-probe needle alignment, which is difficult to achieve precisely.

- Stiffened membranes are stiffer to compression, and therefore have a lower signal. They are however also bending sensitive, as visible in the surrounding taxels.

- Both membrane types show good repeatability for the same stimulus. Variations result from the large impact of variations in the contact point.

Further studies   More experiments were performed on other sensing fingers and taxels, the results are similar but difficult to compare. The sensing behavior is highly dependent on the probe needle - sensor alignment, which is difficult to assess for the integrated sensors. The probe needle also tended to slip over the curved finger surface, further complicating the analysis. The work was therefore focused on the readout of the whole sensing array described in the next section.

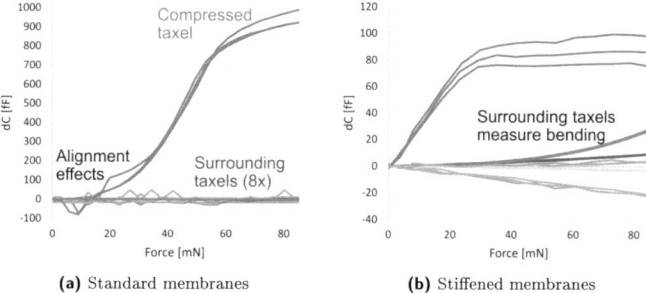

(a) Standard membranes   **(b)** Stiffened membranes

Figure 4.9: Measurement response of standard vs. stiffened membranes. One sensor at the top of the finger is compressed and all surrounding sensors are measured. Each measurement repeated 3x and plotted in the same graph.

4.5 Results - sensing array

While single sensor behavior allows the comparison with previously measured data, the more important experiments are the measurements of the whole sensing finger to stimuli. This section summarizes performed studies.

4.5.1 Experimental setup

The setup was modified to allow the application of larger stimuli. Fig. 4.10 shows a 20 x 10 mm wide stamp connected to a 6-axes forces and moments probe (Rokubi Mini, Bota systems). This probe is not ideal for the set of experiments, as the noise level of ±150 mN is relatively high, resulting in variations of the actual applied force.

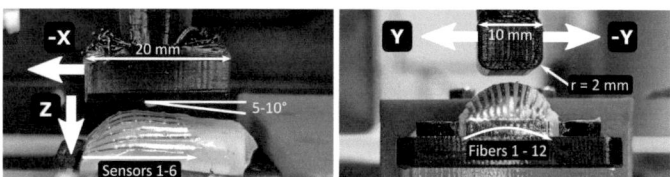

Figure 4.10: Experimental setup for the manipulation of the sensing fingers with a 20x10 mm stamp. [2]

85

4.5.2 Touch and Slide events

Finger F14 was used to study the response to different touch and slide experiments. Fig. 4.11A shows the temporal signal of such an experiment, where a force of 0.5 N was applied on the finger, followed by a waiting period of 4 s and a sliding movement over the finger (in -X direction). At time = 6 s the amplitude and X/Y arrow plots (calculation explained in section 2.4.5) are shown in Fig. 4.11B, giving a better visual understanding of areal effects.

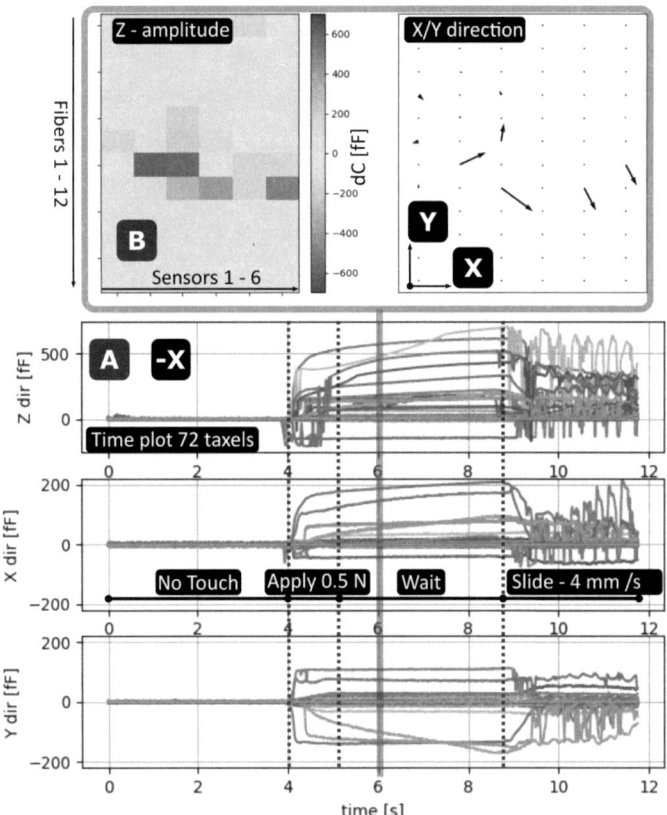

Figure 4.11: Raw data of a touch and slide experiment, showing the taxel responses over time (A) and over area (B). [2]

The amplitude and X/Y plots intuitively make sense when compared with the experimental setup in Fig. 4.10. The finger is slightly tilted (5-10°), resulting in a highest pressure at its tip, and smaller pressure further down in the bulk. The downwards movement results in a sidewards push of the taxels, which is observable in the arrow plots. The temporal signal can be analyzed in its three segments as follows:

1. **Force application:** the force is applied within 1 s, and the taxels first in touch react with a sharp increase in capacitance, easily distinguishable as touch. Some taxels show fluctuations in this period, which are explained further in section 4.5.5.

2. **Waiting:** in this period the applied force is not altered. Signals remain relatively steady, however tend to have a slight drift due to the viscoelastic behavior of the silicone skin. This effect prolongs until the taxels have reached their maximum capacitance, respectively a full deflection.

3. **Sliding:** the sliding movement results in clearly visible oscillations measured by the taxels in contact related to roughness & stick-slip effects between the finger and stamp.

Fig. 4.12A depicts the average values of the X, Y and Z components for sliding the stamp over the finger in different directions (-X as shown in detail in Fig. 4.11 and Y); all camera footage and videos of the areal plots, including experiments in -Y direction, are available in appendix C.1. The plots show how different sliding directions have distinctive features, even though single sensor data is ignored. In -X the stick-slip vibrations are clearly visible, as the stamp slides over the finger for the full movement range. Y/-Y (compare Fig. 4.12 and Fig. C.1) have similar stick-slip effects, however less pronounced, as the stamp loses contact to the finger relatively soon. The sliding direction however can be seen in the average Y curves. It is also possible to extract the direction of movement from the temporal plots of single taxels as visible in Fig. 4.12B, where the taxels of the third vertical column (Fig. 4.11B, first two and last two taxels are ignored) are plotted. The -X plot clearly shows the oscillations as discussed previously, while the Y plot shows how a peak in the capacitance plot moves from taxel to taxel, corresponding to the edge of the stamp sliding over the finger.

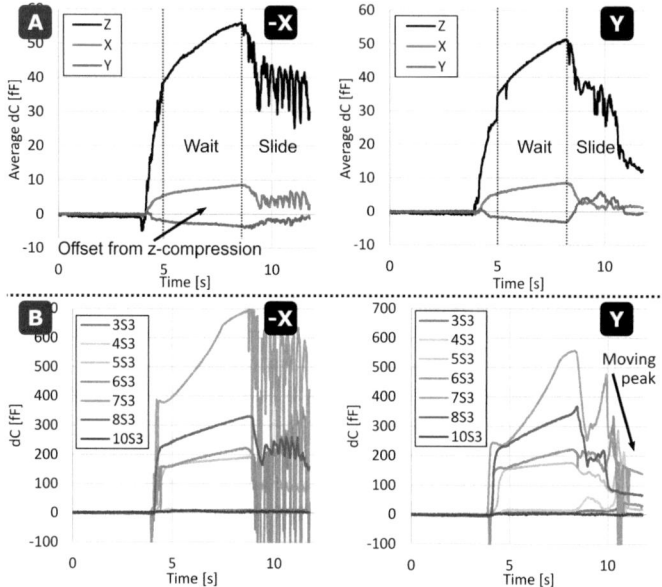

Figure 4.12: A) Averages of all taxel capacitances for touch & slide experiments into various finger directions. B) Single taxel responses of the same experiments along the third column of the sensing array. [2]

4.5.3 Shape & surface distinction

Video https://youtu.be/GrKBsOiF3pg shows the live measurement of an artificial finger when touched by various objects like a ring spanner, sharp scissor edge, different stamps or a human finger. The finger allows shape and surface distinctions by analyzing the combined information of sensors. Shape distinction is shown later in section 4.6.2, where neural networks are used for object classification, based on the tactile images of the sensing finger. Surface distinction can be based on Fourier analysis of vibration patterns as for example shown by [15].

This section describes an initial test, where two stamps with the same shape but different surface roughness are slid over the finger. Fig 4.13 shows the two stamps in comparison. The smooth stamp was covered with a thin layer of leveling epoxy-coating, resulting in a very smooth surface while keeping the same overall shape.

20 mm

Figure 4.13: Rough (left) and smooth (right) surface stamp.

F26 (with stiffened membranes) was used for this investigation, as the signals are less noisy and therefore allow an easier comparison. A similar touch & slide experiment as in Fig. 4.11 was performed, however with 2 N applied force. Fig. 4.14 shows the finger readouts in both cases for all sensors. F26 has a 400 µm thick coating and a stiffened membrane and is therefore less sensitive than the F14.

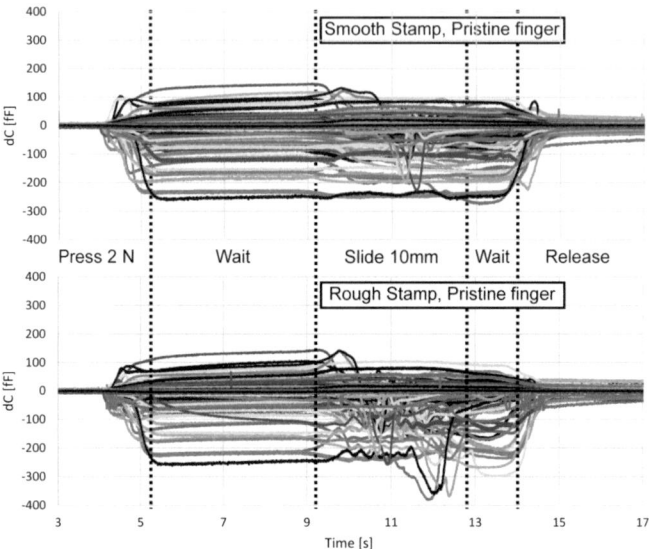

Figure 4.14: Raw readout data of finger (F26) while sliding (-X direction) a smooth and a rough stamp over the finger surface.

The following observations can be made:

- Both stamps result in measured oscillations on the surface. As the smooth stamp has a very low surface roughness, those patterns can be explained with stick-slip between both moving surfaces. This should allow slippage detection, independent of the surface in contact.

- An additional study performed after the endurance test described in the next section investigated the effect of oiling the surface of the smooth stamp versus leaving it as it is. Fig. C.5 compares those results and shows how the sliding is observed with a delay for the oiled surface. Similar observations can be made as a human when sliding over a very smooth and oiled surface, which makes slippage detection more difficult.

- An increased surface roughness results in stronger oscillations. Those kind of patterns should allow surface classification similar as described by [15].

4.5.4 Force estimation & Robustness

Fig. 4.15 summarizes an endurance test on F26 & F30, where a load of 15 N (stage maximum is 20 N) was applied for >2000 times. Fig. C.2 includes the same data for F24 (similar to F30 with slight adaptions) [2]. The capacitance of all 144 taxels is averaged and plotted in 4.15A1 & A2 to show the overall system response. The average capacitances C1 at 5 N & C2 at 14.5 N are taken in each cycle and plotted over the iterations in Fig. 4.15B1 & B2.

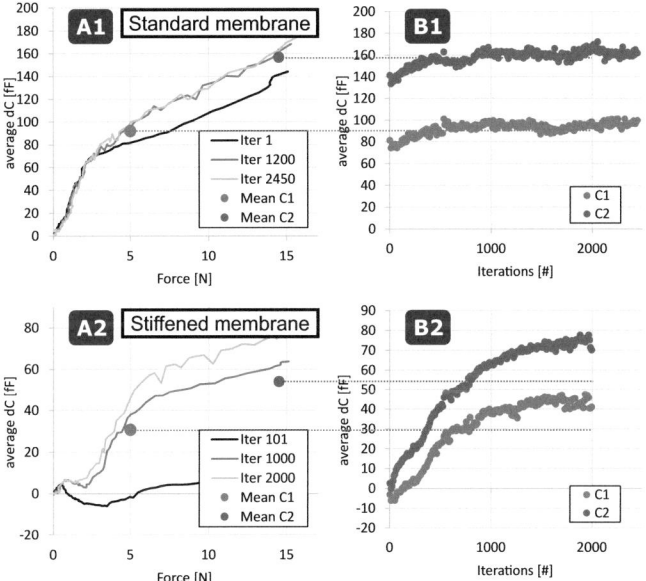

Figure 4.15: Robustness tests: Average of all sensor capacitances for applying forces in the range of 0 - 15 N for >2000 iterations. 1: F30 - standard membrane. 2: F26 - stiffened membrane.

The data allows the following observations:

- Standard and stiffened membranes behave differently. While standard membranes have a short run-in period of ~200 iterations, stiffened membranes take ~1000 iterations until they reach a stable response.

The average capacitance increases. The signals remain stable after the run-in period.

- The average capacitance allows a rough estimation of the applied force (Fig. 4.15A1 & A2). This relationship will depend on the shape of the stamp, which compresses the finger. The artificial finger is therefore no quantitative force sensor, but allows an approximation. It is expected that neural networks might be capable of extracting the applied force with higher accuracy, as they could combine the information with information on the contact area. This is further studied in section 4.6.3.

- Appendix C.2 gives additional information on the performed endurance test, including a movie of the test.

Fig. 4.16 compares Touch&Slide experiments with the smooth stamp on F30 before and after the endurance test, while Fig. 4.17 does the same for F26. The same experiment was repeated for F26 with the rough stamp and can be found in Fig. C.4.

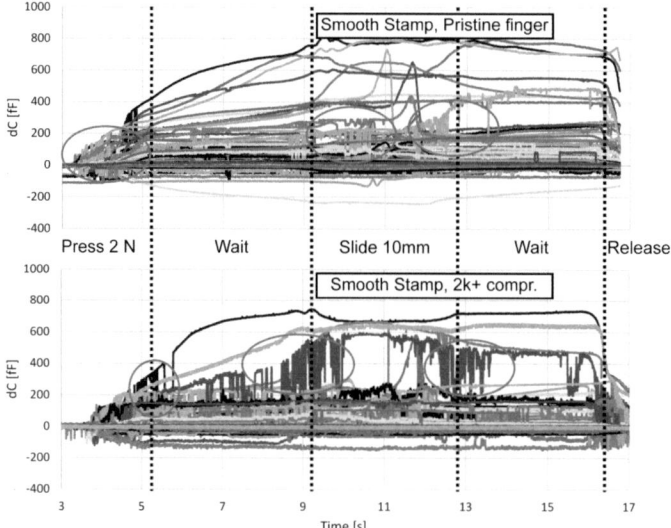

Figure 4.16: Touch & Slide (-X) experiment on F30 (standard membrane) before and after an endurance test with the smooth stamp. Measurement after 2k+ compressions was on slightly different location on the finger. The red circles highlight measurement fluctuations.

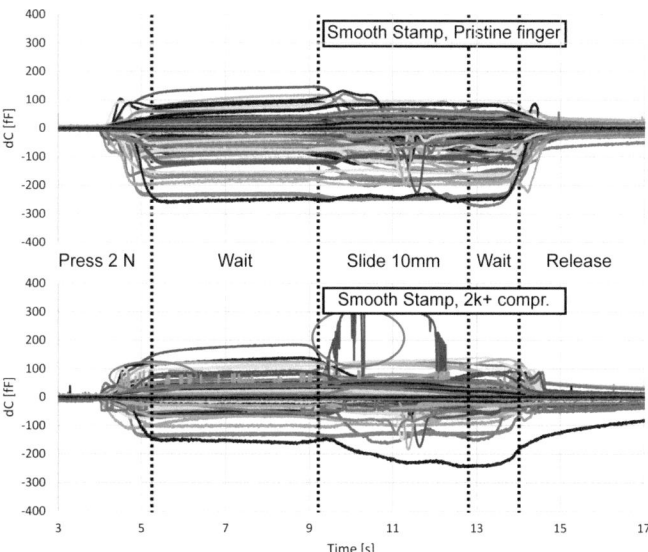

Figure 4.17: Touch & Slide (-X) experiment on F26 (stiffened membrane) before and after an endurance test with the smooth stamp. The red circles highlight measurement fluctuations.

Important observations are:

- Stiffened membranes show significantly less signal fluctuations (in red circles) than the standard membranes, typically already as pristine fingers.

- Stiffened membranes also have less degraded taxels after 2k+ compressions, some fluctuating sensors are however still visible. They therefore seem to be generally more robust to membrane degrading (compare section 4.5.5), show however a less stable response over the compression cycle in Fig. 4.15.

- Standard membranes react mainly to compression and therefore result in positive capacitance changes. Stiffened membranes have a stiffened perimeter and react to a mix of bending and compression. They therefore have sometimes positive, sometimes negative signals, depending on the local load case.

4.5.5 Degradation effects

Some of the sensors show fluctuations, which are expected to result from degradation effects in the taxels respectively the suspended membranes. The following observations resulted in this conclusion:

- The fluctuations already occur in the analog signal as observed by oscilloscope measurements. They are not related to the digital electronics part.

- They are only occuring during finger deformation, but are not observable when no load is applied.

- The effect is observable on single taxels rather than complete lines or rows of the readout matrix, why the electrodes in the flexible substrate can be ruled out as error sources.

- 3E electrodes show all the same fluctuations, why the failure has to be on the supply/membrane side.

Some additional observations are important for a further understanding of the failure mechanism in the membrane:

- The effect is reversible. Signals go back to their initial state if the load on the finger is released.

- Oscilloscope measurements showed that the sinusoidal signal is only decreased. Contacts are therefore weakened, but not broken.

- The stiffened membrane shows less fluctuations over the course of the robustness study. The underflow reduces the strain in the membrane and therefore improves the long-term stability of single taxels.

Fig. 4.18 displays the electrical model used to further explain the degradation effect. The PCB part is introduced in Fig. 5.8, the RC transmission parameters are explained in Tables 2.11 & 2.4. LT Spice simulations were used to investigate the effect of an additional parasitic serial component by the membrane. A parasitic resistance of $R_{Membrane} = 0.1 - 1M\Omega$ or a parasitic capacitance of $C_{Membrane} = 1 - 10pF$ would explain the observed fluctuations. Even larger parasitics would yield signals, which are too small to match the observations. The resistance is more plausible, and can be explained with a weak contact in the membrane sidewalls upon large bending. Further work in this field is necessary to improve the behavior and understanding.

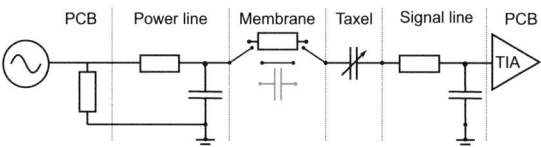

Figure 4.18: Electrical schematic - degradation mechanism

4.6 Neural networks for feature extraction

The large amount of sensor information makes it difficult to do data analysis with classical methods and does not allow to use the full potential of the information richness as shown in the simple experiments in the previous section. The MSc project of Dominik Wojcikiewicz, co-supervised by Mayank Mittal and Firas Farraj from the Robotic Systems Lab (RSL) aimed to analyze the potential of machine learning for the extraction of various features. The most important findings are summarized here.

The study was mainly executed on finger F14 (see Table 4.1). We focused on the extraction of the following features:

- Events: contact, slip & shape distinction

- Contact evaluation: center of contact & total force

Those features were expected to be valuable characteristics for robotic manipulation. This assumption however would still need to be proven in actual robotic studies.

4.6.1 Experimental

Training data was collected with the same setup as in the previously described experiments. The characterization stage was used to apply different stimuli on the artificial finger by varying the applied force, location of contact, movement direction for slipping experiments or also the sequence of different mechanical stimuli for robustness analyses. Additionally, we used different stamps depicted in Fig. 4.19 to test the capabilities of shape recognition.

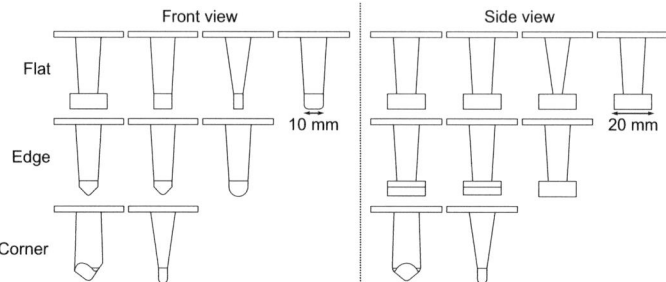

Figure 4.19: 3d printed tips that were attached to the Rokubi force sensor for data acquisition. Tips are split into different classes that were predicted in the shape recognition task in 4.6.2.

Test data was generated by fixing the Rokubi force probe in a vice and moving the artificial finger manually as depicted in Fig. 4.20. This method was used to test the robustness of the trained neural networks to imperfect actuation, which is much more relevant to the final use case.

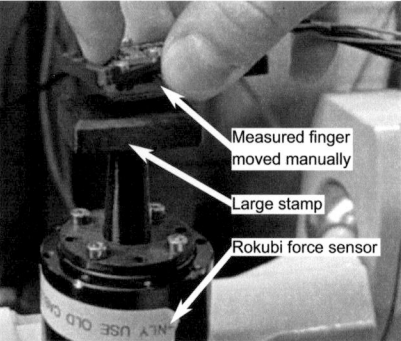

Figure 4.20: Manual measurement setup. The artificial finger is moved by hand and the force probe with a large stamp is fixed in a vice. Adapted from [69].

The force probe was used to define labels for the training data. The relative large noise level of ± 150 mN complicated the detection of fine contact events and introduced delays due to the necessary thresholds.

4.6.2 Event and shape detection by classification

The data in this section is better understandable when watching the video
https://youtu.be/aRm_vVQCqWs, which contains videos of the setup and
results.

Contact detection worked very well with accuracies around 95% or higher.
the network does not misinterpret the viscoelastic behavior of the silicone
resulting in a fade-out of the sensor signal after the release of contact. It
is therefore much more robust than a simple heuristic of averaging sensor
signals and defining a threshold. Inaccuracies at the start and end of contact
sequences originate from problems with the ground truth labelling due to
force probe noise.

The same experiment was used for shape recognition. The large stamp shown
in Fig. 4.20 was used to detect the contact with the flat surface, edge or
corner. Fig. 4.21 shows the confusion matrix of this experiment.

	Ratio [%]	Actual event			
		NC	Flat	Edge	Corner
Predicted event	No Contact	41.0	1.1	2.3	1.7
	Flat	0.1	12.3	1.2	0.0
	Edge	1.3	0.6	23.6	2.7
	Corner	0.6	0.0	1.0	9.6	Total
	Accuracy [%]	95.2	87.5	84.2	68.8	87.3

Figure 4.21: Confusion matrix - contact and shape detection. Experiment of
45s, ∼9800 tactile frames (consult video for better understanding).
Data based on [69].

Shape recognition therefore worked with good detection accuracies, except
for the corner detection. It was however expected that this behavior could be
improved with more training data on the manual setup, as the training data
on the characterization setup was not ideal for simulating corner contact at
the sidewalls of the finger, as only z-movements were possible.

Slip detection worked originally well on the controlled setup (∼95%), the
accuracy however dropped in the manual tests (∼83%). This decline was
mainly expected to relate to the degradation of the sensor signals over the
course of the project. More robust sensors are important for a reliable detec-

tion. The detection of slip was the only feature in this project which showed higher detection accuracies when three-dimensional sensing data of the 3E sensors was activated. Detection accuracy was 92.4% without activated 3D sensing data and 95.7% with activated sensing data. It was not evaluated however if a higher density of 1E sensors (DL array) might improve the detection accuracy in the same way.

4.6.3 Force and location measurement by regression

Another video `https://youtu.be/7PK_OssUNNs` summarizes the results of this section and is highly recommended for a better understanding of the results.

The approximation of the contact force proved to be possible for different types of contacts (surface, edge, corner) with a root mean square (RMS) error of ∼0.3 N. This data is not comparable with the accurate results of a dedicated force sensor, which was however expected.

The location of contact could be estimated with an RMS error of ∼1.1 mm, which is reasonable for an approximate sensor spacing of 2 x 2 mm on this finger. This experiment was evaluated in the manual setup and the ground truth manually labelled by studying the video recordings. Detection would be more accurate in a controlled setup, but it would not be representative because the current setup only includes three axes.

4.7 Summary of capabilities and open questions

Sections 4.5 & 4.6 summarized some preliminary studies, which could be performed on the sensing finger. Some measurement capabilities are well observable by direct signal analysis like the detection of events (touch & slide), simple shapes, effects of different contact surfaces or a rough estimation of the contact force. The neural network - based studies could confirm and further quantify those capabilities. All features could be extracted with agreeable to good scores even on the early finger F14, which degraded significantly over the course of the project, proving the robustness of neural-network based feature extraction. Much future work is however necessary to test robustness, device-to-device performance and the extraction of even more features.

Two important open questions still need to be investigated in further detail however:

- Degradation of sensor signals: the sensor signals of the used fingers degrade as discussed in section 4.5.5. While the fluctuations are reversible and still allow an overall similar finger response over time (see Fig. 4.15, especially case 1), it is problematic for events, where dynamic signal analysis is important. This could be observed as lower achievable scores in slippage detection in the later stages of the feature extraction studies.

  The effect was characterized and a plausible explanation found. There are multiple methods, which can be explored to optimize this behavior:

  1. The membrane design and process can be adapted to avoid stress peaks, increasing their robustness.

  2. The packaging process can be adapted to further reduce the stress in the membrane. A simple approach would be an increased skin thickness.

  3. The finger geometry can be adapted to decrease bending effects in the finger geometry. Early studies showed, that stiff finger bulks show much less fluctuations in sensor signals.

  The results displayed for the stiffened membrane were first attempts towards more robust sensors. Table 4.2 compares the standard and stiffened membranes.

  Stiffened membranes result in partially negative sensor responses. While this complicates the definition of an analytical model, a final learning algorithm should not be influenced by this. It remains to be seen which sensor types are better suited for the application, and if the effects can be combined to a better overall sensor.

- The information extracted from the soft fingers is generally less accurate than in rigid sensing systems, which can be calibrated much easier. The generated information has a fuzzy character, and would need to be combined with suitable controllers. Ultimately this should however still allow robust robotic manipulation, as the human counterpart is capable of doing exactly that.

Both points raise the question of how valuable the very soft fingertip is, as it comes with drawbacks. A conclusive answer could not be given in the course of this thesis and would need further studies close to an application.

Table 4.2: Comparison of standard and stiffened membranes.

Membrane type	Standard	Stiffened
Measures	Compression	Bending & Compression (Fig. 4.9)
Single taxel robustness	Lower	Higher, less fluctuations in single taxels (Fig. 4.17)
Overall signal amplitude stability	Better	Worse (Fig. 4.15)
Sensitivity	Slightly higher	Slightly lower (Fig. 4.9)
3D sensing capabilities	Better	Worse, sensor tilt blocked by stiffened membrane perimeter (tested on different fingers).
Model simplicity	Easier	Worse, underflow effect difficult to describe.

5 Characterization setup & Electronics

This chapter describes the measurement setup used for most of the sensor and finger characterization experiments as well as the electronics for the sensor readout. The setup is introduced, followed by a mechanical characterization. The different iterations of electronics are introduced, including a section about the interpretation of measurement errors. Finally, the programming approach is presented.

5.1 General overview

Fig. 5.1 displays the characterization setup, configured with EV2 (*Electronics Version 2*, see section 5.3) electronics and for the characterization of sensors on a chip. The flowchart in Fig. 5.2 further summarizes the communication paths between all elements of the setup. The mechanical structure consists of a structure out of laser-cut MDF wooden plates with the following components:

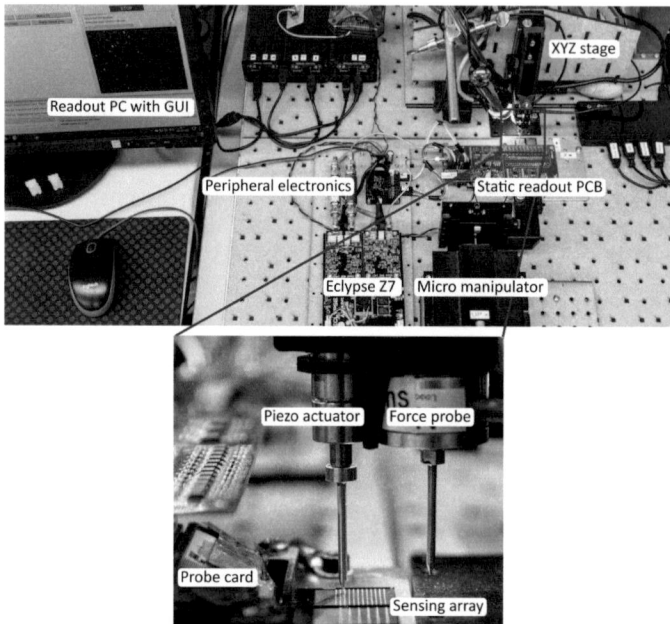

Figure 5.1: Characterization setup with a close-up of the measurement area and its characterization probes. [2]

- Stage: XYZ stage with high resolution stepper motors (Standa, X/Y resolution = 0.3 µm, Z resolution = 0.16 µm).

- Force probes: two versions existed.

  - High resolution force probe for sensor characterization: Novatech F329 with a resolution of 50 µN and a range of 100 mN. An aluminum needle is attached to the force probe, which is coated with a 5 µm thick parylene layer to avoid interference with the electrical measurements.

  - Large range force sensor: Rokubi Mini force sensor with a resolution of ~300 mN and a range of 200 N. Different 3D-printed stamps were attached to it for finger characterizations.

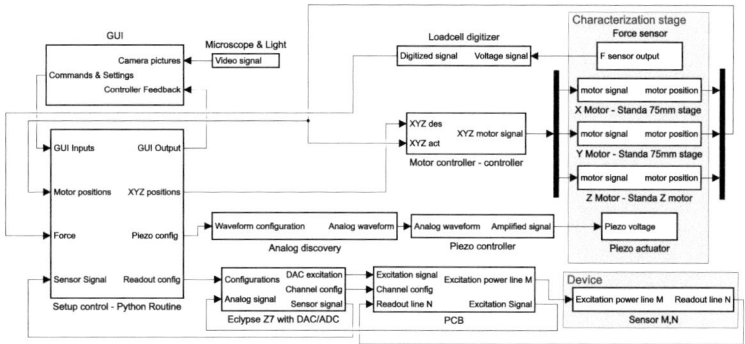

Figure 5.2: Flow chart of the components in the characterization setup.

- Piezo actuation stage: for applying dynamic stimuli or very small deflections. It consists of the Analog Discovery 2 (AD2) for the wave generation, the piezo controller and piezo actuator. The measurement principle was introduced in section 3.3.4.1.

- Micromanipulator: The contact pads of the sensor array are contacted with a needle probe card, which is aligned with a manual micromanipulator.

- Microscope: with video feed to the graphical user interface (GUI) for the optical alignment of probes and samples.

- Readout electronics: different versions further introduced in section 5.3.

- Measurement PC: PC with a python routine for the control of the setup and a GUI.

5.2 Mechanical aspects of the setup

The setup was used to measure static and dynamic characteristics. The measurements are to some extent influenced by the setup itself and need to be compensated or eliminated.

5.2.1 Static measurements and system stiffness

The high resolution force probe has a non-negligible softness, which influences the measurement of force-displacement (FD) curves. An applied force on one side deforms the sensor and on the other side the used force probe. The measured displacement change therefore needs to be compensated.

The system stiffness was measured in the course of the Master thesis project by Lorenz Kehrbein. We found that small metallic balls (0.8 mm diameter) as depicted in Fig. 5.3 are an ideal way to measure the system stiffness. Flat surfaces result in artifacts at very small forces, as the needle surface and reference surface first need to align, resulting in calibration errors.

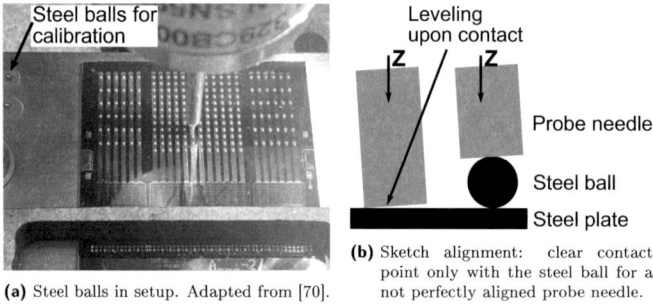

(a) Steel balls in setup. Adapted from [70].

(b) Sketch alignment: clear contact point only with the steel ball for a not perfectly aligned probe needle.

Figure 5.3: Mechanical calibration of the setup with steel balls.

The extracted system compliance is setup-dependent and was used in all measurements shown in this report to convert the measured displacement into a compensated displacement as for example visible in Fig. 4.1b. The accuracy still depends on the z-axis accuracy of the motor, which is 1.5 μm (supplier data).

5.2.2 Dynamic measurements and system eigenfrequency

Each mechanical system can be simplified into a system of masses and springs and has at least one eigenfrequency. This was relevant for the dynamic excitation of sensors with the piezoactuator, as the probe head can be seen as a mass connected to the stage with a holder of finite stiffness. The old probe head shown on the left in Fig. 5.4a resulted in the dynamic sensor responses shown in Fig. 5.5a. It is visible that all sensors show a resonance peak around 350 Hz, which could be explained as a resonance peak of the setup. A new, stiffer probe holder (Fig. 5.4b) was designed and the frequency spectrum measured with this holder is compared with an old one in Fig. 5.5b. The stiffer probe holder has a resonance peak at around 750 Hz, which is outside of the investigated spectrum of 0 - 500 Hz. This new holder was used for all experiments presented in this thesis. If broader frequency analyses are necessary, an additional modification of the probe holder or z-axis stage needs to be considered.

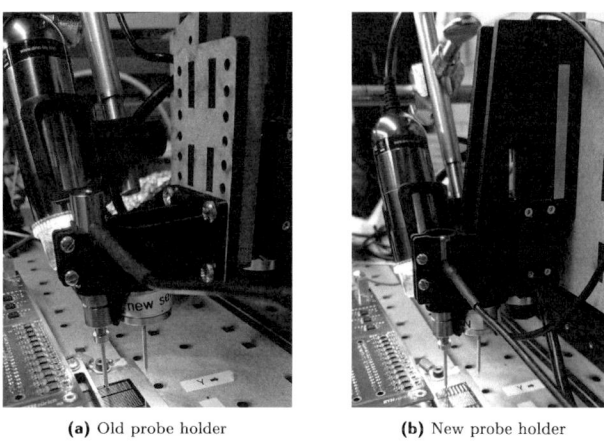

(a) Old probe holder   (b) New probe holder

Figure 5.4: Probe heads for the fixing of the static and dynamic probes.

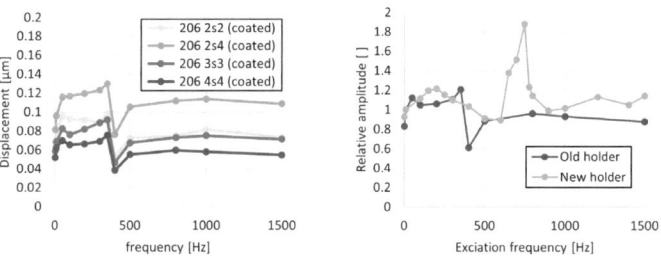

(a) Measurements on four sensors with old probe head, adapted from [71].

(b) Measurements with old and new probe head compared (on different sensors).

Figure 5.5: Influence of the eigenfrequency on dynamic measurements and optimization.

5.3 Architectures of the electrical readout of sensors

Four versions of electrical readout systems were used over the course of this work. Results in [1] were measured with EV0 (*Electronics Version*), [47] used EV1 and [2] EV2 & EV3.

5.3.1 EV0 - LCR meter

In [1,47] a precision LCR meter (Agilent 4284A) read out the sensor capacitance. The contacting is done with a dedicated cable offering two clamps, which are attached to the probe card plug outputs manually. The contacts of those clamps proved to be unreliable and small movements could result in large fluctuations of the actual measured capacitance. The system was therefore not suitable to measure the nominal capacitance of the sensors (which was mainly influenced by the cabling and contacts), but only relative capacitance changes during a stable mechanical connection. The Pro's and Con's of this setup are summarized in table 5.1. The same setup was used to measure calibration capacitances for EV1-3. Those measurements were performed with another dedicated clamp, which was more reliable.

Table 5.1: Pro's and con's of EV0

Pro's	Con's
Simple setup	Readout of only one sensor possible (reclamping of contacts for different sensor).
	Instability of mechanical contacts, large parasitic effect.

5.3.2 EV1 - Analog discovery

EV1 was developed in collaboration with Marcel Ott (Semester project), Thomas Burger and Thomas Kleier and was described in [47]. Fig. 5.6 shows the block diagram for the readout of the sensors.

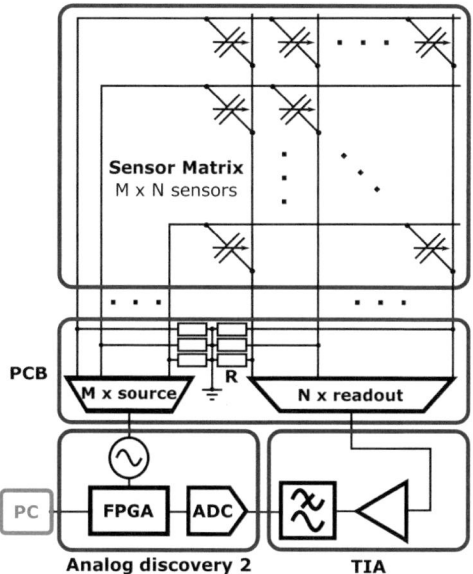

Figure 5.6: Block diagram of EV1. [47]

The main elements are:

- AD2 oscilloscope: generation of a sinusoidal excitation and digitization of the feedback signal.

- PCB: address the individual sensors by multiplexing.

- Transimpedance amplifier (TIA, FEMTO DHPCA-100): amplification and low pass filtering of the sensor signal.

The main components on the PCB are the multiplexers (74HC4067PW) as well as R = 1 kΩ resistors to ground on every source and readout line. The resistors remove injected charge on the not activated source/readout lines, thereby avoiding crosstalk between sensor rows. The signal path is designed as follows:

1. A sinusoidal voltage is generated in the AD2.

2. The voltage is routed to source line M in the source multiplexer.

3. The source voltage generates a current that flows through sensor $C_{M,N}$, which is selected by the readout demultiplexer by connecting readout line N.

4. The current is converted back to voltage and filtered in the TIA stage, which then

5. is sampled by the AD2 and sent to the computer for post processing.

A computer program controls the sensor array switching operation and computes the signal amplitude at the excitation frequency using fast Fourier transform (FFT). This general measurement principle is described as an auto-balancing bridge method in [72] to measure impedances; the change of impedance, derived from the amplitude, is the sensor signal.

5.3.2.1 Characterization

Table 5.2 shows a selection of parameters and characteristics of the measurement configuration. The sensitivity was evaluated by measuring the readout response (change of signal amplitude in V) of several capacitors between 0.5 - 1.5 pF and a linear relationship could be confirmed with a coefficient of determination of $R^2 = 0.9999$. Each capacitor was measured 100 times and the resolution was defined as the

$$RMS_{Noise} = \sqrt{1/N \sum_{n=1}^{N}(C_n - \overline{C})^2} \qquad (5.1)$$

Table 5.2: EV1: important parameters and characteristics. [47]

Description	Unit	Value
Excitation frequency	kHz	300
Update rate between sensors	kHz	5
Sensitivity	fF/V	3860.9
Resolution	fF	1.4

The resolution depends on the readout time per sensor; a lower update rate allows for a better resolution by longer signal acquisition. A comparison of the measurements with EV0 and EV1 was previously shown in Fig. 2.31, showing that both systems measure the same signal.

Fig. 5.7 shows the readout of the first two rows of a 6 x 6 sensor array while actuating the sensor at the coordinates (2, 2). The graph displays the measurement results of the 12 sensors, showing that only the actuated sensor displays a measurement response, while all other sensors show no change in signal. Previous experiments proved that resistor arrays to ground (compare Fig. 5.6) on all source and readout lines are essential to eliminate crosstalk between sensors on the same source or readout lines by suppressing floating potentials due to charge injection. This design was adapted for all future electronics.

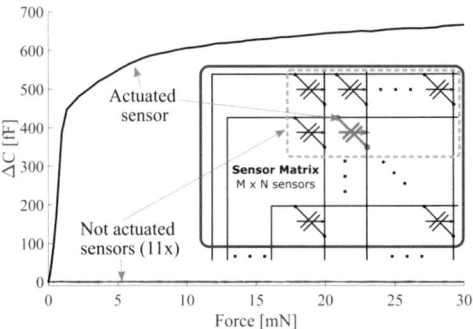

Figure 5.7: Measurement of electrical crosstalk in the sensor array. No crosstalk can be observed after the inclusion of the resistor arrays. [47]

5.3.3 EV2 & EV3 - FPGA based readout

All measurements in [2] and chapters 3 & 4 were performed with EV2 respectively EV3. These electronics were developed in collaboration with Pragash Sivananthanaguru (MSc thesis, details can be found in [73]) and Thomas Burger. The analog part of the readout electronics is based in its principles on EV1 with the adaption of having the charge amplifier placed for each readout line before the multiplexer to improve sensitivity and signal conditioning. The signal analysis and processing part were reworked to allow a fast readout of the sensor arrays and hereby real-time applications. Fig. 5.8 shows the overall concept of the readout electronics with the three major components:

1. Sensing array

2. PCB: for signal routing and amplification

3. the Eclypse Z7 board (Digilent): with DAC and ADC cards with 100 MHz sampling rates as well as the Zynq 7020 System on Chip (SoC) with a dual core processor and a FPGA.

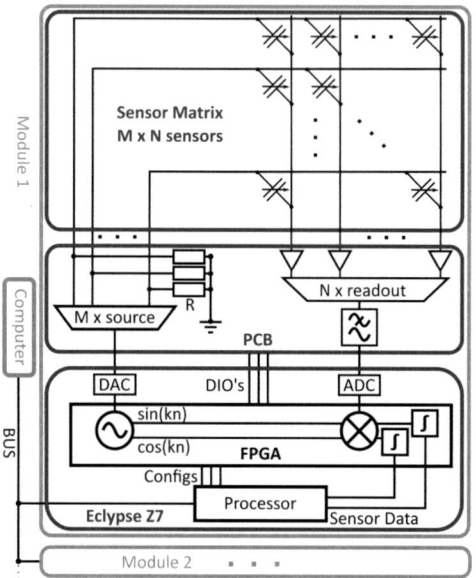

Figure 5.8: Block diagram of EV2. [2]

5.3.3.1 EV2 & EV3 - differences in the readout PCB

The readout PCB comes in two versions, which have the same functionality but some different characteristics as summarized in table 5.3.

Table 5.3: Characteristics of EV2 & EV3

	EV2	EV3
Description	Stationary PCB	Small PCB integrated on artificial finger
Picture reference	Fig. 5.1	Fig. 4.7
Readout channels	12 x 24	12 x 12
Connection to sensing array	probe card for the chip readout	FFC connector to flexible sensing array

5.3.3.2 IQ mixer

The FPGA has an implemented IQ mixer [74]. The 1.5625 MHz sinusoidal signal for the sensor excitation is generated with a CORDIC algorithm on the FPGA and fed to the DAC but also as a sine & cosine to the signal mixer. The signal, which went through the sensor matrix is sampled with the ADC and then multiplied with the sine and cosine signal to deliver the I and Q parts of the readout signal. When reading out the sensor array the following steps are carried out:

1. the digital outputs of the FPGA are changed to switch to a specific taxel,

2. a timer waits for a defined settling time,

3. the integrators for the I & Q parts of the signal are started and

4. stopped when switching to the next taxel.

The I & Q values are sent to the processor where they are summarized as

$$A = \sqrt{I^2 + Q^2}, \tag{5.2}$$

which is the amplitude of the signal generated by that specific taxel. This amplitude is linear to the capacitance of the taxel and is calibrated. The sensitivity is 5528.7 fF / V. The signal integration combined with the IQ mixer acts as a very narrow bandpass filter at the excitation frequency as shown in Fig. 5.9. The filter quality depends on the number of integrated periods, a longer measurement time results in a lower noise level.

111

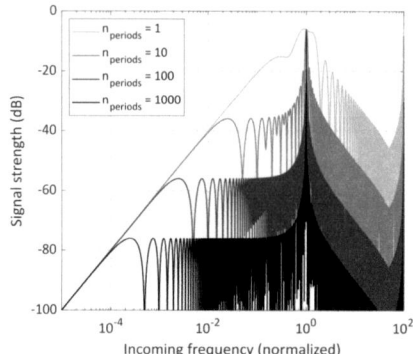

Figure 5.9: IQ mixer filter characteristic. Filter characteristic of the implemented IQ mixer for different integration times (number of integrated periods). [2]

5.3.3.3 Characterization

Fig. 5.10a shows the average measured resolution RMS_{Noise} (see equation 5.1) in relation to the sensor update frequency (1.25 kHz was used for single taxel characterizations, 31 kHz for finger readout experiments).

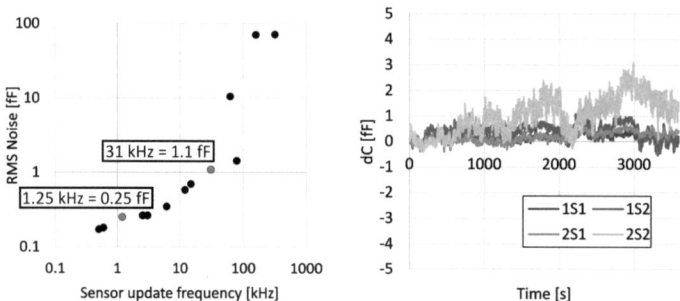

(a) Average RMS noise level of 144 sensors for different sensor update frequencies.

(b) Drift of the first four sensors in an array over 1h measurement time.

Figure 5.10: Results EV3. [2]

Another important criterion for longer measurements is a low drift of the sensors and readout electronics, which is often observed in resistive sensor types and was one of the main reasons to aim for capacitive taxels in this work. Fig. 5.10b shows the drift of the first four taxels of an array over 1h measurement time with relatively low fluctuations of -0.5 - 2.5 fF.

5.3.4 Summary

Table 5.4 summarizes the key performance parameters of the different electronics versions.

Table 5.4: Comparison of the electronic readout versions

	EV0	EV1	EV2	EV3
Channels	1 x 1	8 x 16	12 x 24	12 x 12
Resolution [fF]	nA	1.4 @ 5kHz	Slightly worse than EV3	1.1 @ 30 kHz 0.25 @ 1.25 kHz
Continous read-out possible	No	No	Yes	Yes
Sensing array movable during measurement	No	No	No	Yes
Long-term stability	No	Yes	Yes	Yes

This information can now be combined with the measured sensitivities between 220 - 660 μm (Fig. 3.6) times the sensitivity ratio S_R (Fig. 4.5) for the taxel sensitivity on the finger to calculate the force resolution of the taxels as shown in Table 5.5. Choosing a 31 kHz update rate (~217 Hz for a 144-sensor array) a skin thickness between 440-660 μm results in a force resolution of ~0.1-0.2 mN per taxel. This is expected to be ideal for the artificial finger, as the force resolution is 5 - 10 times smaller than for a human finger (sensing range 1-10 kPa [7] and Meissner cell density $\sim 1\ sensor/mm^2$).

Table 5.5: Possible force resolution of EV3 for taxels integrated on a finger with different skin thicknesses. [2]

Coating behavior		Force resolution Finger	
Thickness [μm]	**Sensitivity [fF/mN]**	**31kHz [mN]**	**1.25kHz [mN]**
220	24.75	0.04	0.01
440	12.3	0.09	0.02
660	6.12	0.18	0.04

5.4 Typical failure modes and their characteristics

The typical sensor curve was introduced in Fig. 2.31, however there are multiple reasons why sensors do not show this ideal behavior which are summarized in Fig. 5.11. Table 5.6 summarizes all typical failure modes for wrong sensor measurements including explanations and approaches to eliminate the problems. The network stabilizer used to eliminate failure mode 6 is shown in Fig. B.3.

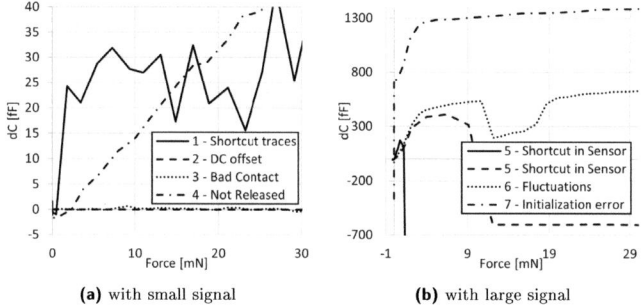

(a) with small signal

(b) with large signal

Figure 5.11: Typical failed measurements with small and large signal effects.

Table 5.6: Measurement failure modes and explanations.

Case	Observations	Area of effect	Problem	Root cause	Solution	Frequency of observation
1 - Shortcut traces	Characteristic curve looks like a very weak Taxel with high and low sensitivity region.	Several lines/rows in sensing array	Shortcut between readout lines in flexible substrate, signal is grounded hereby.	Flexible substrate	Reduce particle defects in fabrication	Rare
2 - DC offset	Signal stays at 0 fF for the measurement, maybe fluctuates slightly. ADC signal has large DC offset and signal is in one of the rails. No amplitude signal therefore (pure DC)	One line/row of sensing array	Low ohmic contact (<100 Ohm) from source/readout line to GND. Happens due to particle defects in the fabrication.	Flexible substrate	Reduce particle defects in fabrication	Rare
3 - Bad Contact	ADC signal is very small, but with measurable signal.	One line/row of sensing array	Bad connection between sensing array and probe needle array	Measurement technique	Realigning of probe needles can solve the problem. However it is often difficult to get all probe needles in reliable contact at once	Often
4 - Not Released	Linear but low increase of dC for increasing force	One Taxel	Taxels are not released or sticking on the stopper structures	Taxel	Taxel fabrication issue. Fabrication failure (or not ideal taxel type).	Rare (for good designs)
5 - Shortcut in Taxel	Signal collapses after initially good characteristic	One Taxel	Shortcut between membrane and electrodes	Taxel	Improvement in Taxel design, problem solved.	Extinct (for good designs)
6 - Fluctuations	Signal randomly switches between various levels	Random	Fluctuations in network supply / ground loops expected	Measurement technique	Solved by using a network stabilizer and breaking up ground loops	Extinct
7 - Initialization error	Large variations in initial capacitance	Random	Initialization error on the FPGA, first value of wrong amplitude	Measurement technique	Improved FPGA readout initialization, which was implemented	Extinct

5.4.1 Explanations with raw signal

The FPGA allows to directly log the DAC and ADC signals in another measurement mode (mode 1 in the GUI). Fig. 5.12 shows such loggings with two traces of ADC signals, where twelve sensors were measured in a row with 312 kHz switching frequency between sensors. This method can be used to investigate the root cause of measurement failures:

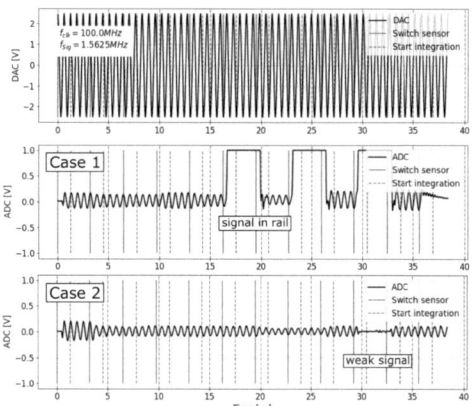

Figure 5.12: Sensor raw signals. Top: DAC output signal, Mid & Bottom: ADC measurement of 12 sensors, showing different defects.

- Case 1: shows how the ADC signal is stuck in the rail, what corresponds to failure mode 2 (DC offset).

- Case 2: shows a weak signal (failure mode 3) on one of the sensors.

Other failure modes generally show a sinusoidal signal and are therefore less distinctive. Those failure modes can only be identified by longer time period observations, which were done with an oscilloscope.

5.4.2 Imperfections in 3E sensors

A measurement imperfection, which is often found in 3E sensors, are variations in the maximum capacitance between all electrodes as visible in Fig. 5.13. This is not seen as an actual measurement error, as it is mainly related to a non-ideal alignment of the probe needle and taxel, resulting in a tilted sensor. A realignment can solve this imperfection, which is however tedious in automatic sensing array readouts.

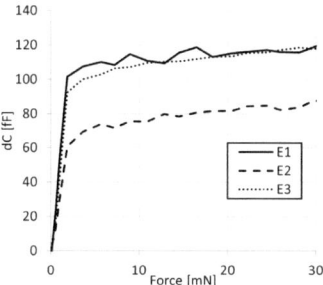

Figure 5.13: 3E sensor measurement with different maximum capacitances.

5.5 Programming approach

More than 100k measurements were executed on the characterization setup. This was only possible due to the high degree of automation, which is introduced in this section. The program is written in Python and has the following main building blocks:

- Widgetsdef script: Defines the functionality of all measurement routines (widgets). It's the core function accessing all other components.

- Drivers: Each component in the system has its own driver file, which allows to send high-level commands from the main script.

- GUI script: script defining the GUI and its functionalities. It is embedded in Widgetsdef.

The code base is maintained in GitHub and a ReadMe includes further information for new users. Several students (Bruna Azevedo, Marcell Ott, Lorenz Kehrbein, Pragash Sivananthanaguru, Felix Mähr, Curdin Cavelti, Dominik Wojcikiewicz) worked on the improvement of functionalities.

117

5.5.1 GUI overview

Fig. 5.14 shows an overview on the GUI with its main elements. The GUI is structured in seven main tabs:

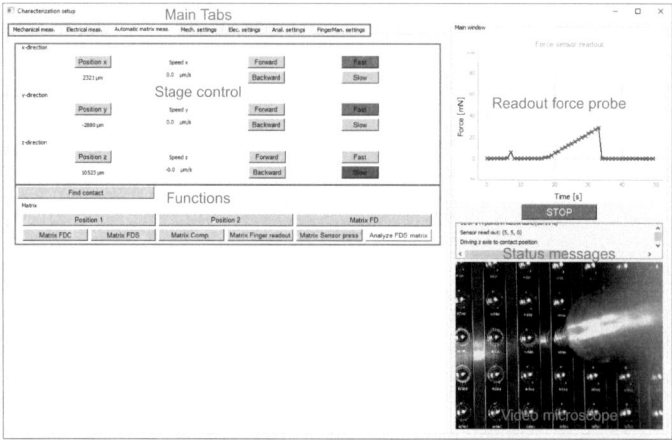

Figure 5.14: GUI overview with the automatic matrix measurement tab open

- Mechanical measurements: mechanical manipulation of sensors, stage movements, etc.

- Electrical measurements: Readout of the taxels/arrays, live streams of sensor array readouts, etc.

- Automatic matrix measurements: Functions, where all taxels of a matrix are measured automatically. The user defines the first and last location of the sensing matrix and the location of all taxels is calculated from it.

- Settings tabs: Mechanical, Electrical, Analytical, Finger Manipulation. Those parameter lists allow the modification of measurement scripts for different scenarios. Fig. B.2 shows an example setting tab.

5.5.2 Databases

All measurement data is saved in SQL databases, which are structured in different tables depending on the executed measurement script. Fig. 5.15 shows a screenshot of a few lines from a database. Each measurement is labelled with a given name and the measurement time stamp. The database contains all measurement settings, the measurement data and various analyses on the measurement depending on defined readout modes.

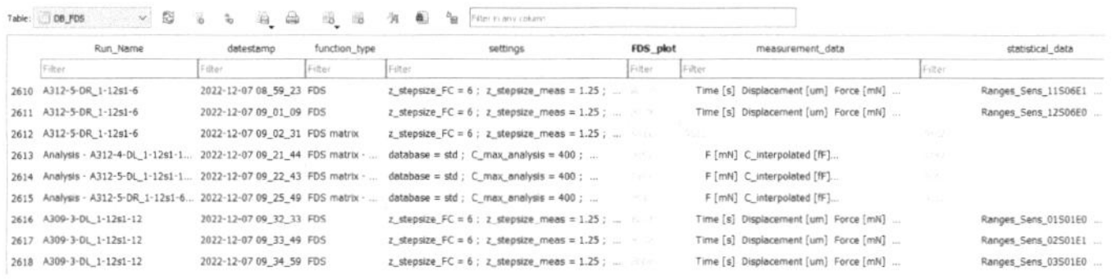

Figure 5.15: Database output. A few lines of the database output of automatic matrix measurements are displayed.

The database approach allowed a well-structured storage of measurement data in an environment easily queried by different programs. This simplified the analysis of sensor matrix readouts, sensing array traces for neural network training and other tasks.

6 Conclusion

6.1 Final evaluation and comparison with other technologies

Table 1.2 summarized the goals defined for this thesis and showed how other technologies perform in the defined criteria. The results of this thesis are evaluated in table 6.1. The sensing technology shows promising capabilities when compared with the other technologies and the drawbacks identified in table 1.3 can be omitted. The overall advantage of sensing skins is the better adaptivity to small bodies due to their small form factor. Additionally, the proposed technology can cover an arbitrary object, either by changing the shape and length of the sensing fibers or by superposing several sensing arrays for even higher sensor density, as the thickness of one flexible substrate is in the range of 10 - 20 µm.

The sensing capabilities of the taxels to static and dynamic touch are proven when integrated in a soft material and supported with simulations. An important design element is the silicone skin thickness, which allows an easy tailoring of system sensitivity and/or robustness. Sensitivities between 2.6 - 0.035 kPa^{-1} could be demonstrated for skin thicknesses between 0 - 660 µm. A skin thickness of 440 - 660 µm is expected to be ideal for the artificial finger, as the force resolution is 5 - 10 times smaller than for a human finger (see section 5.3.4). The sensors were also capable of measuring vibrations in a range of 0 - 500 Hz without loss of signal strength, the overall sensitivity however depends on the skin thickness. 3D sensing capabilities could be proven qualitatively for unpackaged and packaged taxels.

Another important aspect of the taxels is their low susceptibility to noise:

- There is no electronic crosstalk between taxels of the array.

- They do not react differently to different approaching surfaces (non-conductive, conductive/grounded surfaces and permanent magnets tested, see videos `https://youtu.be/GrKBsOiF3pg` & `https://youtu.be/h6BnH82u8t4`).

Table 6.1: Overview achievements compared to the goals defined in table 1.2.

	Criteria	Range/Goal	Achievements	Open questions	Discussed in section:
Sensing	**Pressure Range**	1 - 10 kPa	Proven. Modifiable by skin thickness. 2.6 - 0.035 kPa^{-1} tested		2.4.4.3, 3.3.3, 5.3.4
	Spatial resolution	1 mm touch, 3 mm vibration	Proven		2.1
	Frequency range	0-500 Hz	Proven		3.3.4
	Strain / Shear sensing	No quantitative data for humans	Proven qualitatively	Detailed characterization	2.4.5 4.5.2
Integration	**Integration 3D finger**	Applicability to human sized finger (L/ W/ H = 25 / 15 / 10 mm)	Partially proven	Sensing on full finger periphery needs array modification	4.3
	Compliance	Human-like	Partially proven	Only optimized for finger center	4.1
	Electrical interfaces	Reliability and simplicity	Partially proven	Downsizing to chip level	5.3
	Manufacturing and Cost	Minimized	Estimation: 50-100 CHF for 10k devices/year 20-40 for 100k dev/year	Optimization of processes for lower cost & higher yield.	2.5
Reliability	**Mechanical Robustness**	Application dependent, no standards	Stable for 2k iter @ 15N	Robustness to be optimized/proven depending on use case	4.5.3
	Susceptibility to noise	No crosstalk from electromagnetic (EM) /thermal noise, no drift	No taxel crosstalk, thermal range 20-80°C, no influence of different surfaces or strong electromagnetic fields from a motor (40A current). Low drift over time.	Further characterization of large electromagnetic noise influence.	2.4.7 5.3.2.1 5.3.3.3

- No interference from closeby noisy cables (USB 3.0 dataline) or strong electromagnetic waves from direct drive motors (40A peak current) could be observed (video `https://youtu.be/h6BnH82u8t4`).

Noise behavior will still need to be examined more quantitatively. The sensors also showed a reasonably stable response between 20 - 80°C (section 2.4.7), and long term measurements over an hour a very low drift of <2.5 fF (Fig. 5.10b).

The bulk finger integration was an important step to prove the applicability of the sensing technology. The complete soft integration of the taxels modifies their very defined characteristics, and single sensor data ceases to be as relevant when compared to the whole sensor array in the artificial finger. A soft, human-like finger bulk is expected to be advantageous in real applications, even though it complicates the sensor readout and interpretation:

- The finger surface is more adaptable to different shapes and increases the contact area, allowing better object manipulation.

- A softer bulk should make the sensing finger more robust, as the bulk can more easily compensate for punctual forces or impacts.

Several studies were performed on the integrated finger. Events like touch and slip were analyzed, the compression response investigated over a cyclic loading and deterioration mechanisms investigated. The taxels show degradation over time, which is expected to result from relatively large bending within the soft, artificial finger. First attempts towards more robust taxels were started and reasonably stable responses over 2000 iterations with 15 N applied force could be shown. We studied how feature extraction with neural networks allows to extract simple features from the large datastream of the sensing array. First results were promising, as we could detect contact, slipping and the shape of simple structures with good accuracies of $\sim 90\%$. The networks also allowed an estimation of the contact force and contact location. The results are very promising, as they showed the robustness of this approach even for an early, strongly degrading artificial finger.

6.1.1 Comparison with the human tactile sense

It is possible to conclude from the experiments, that the proposed and integrated capacitive taxels can track all mechanical stimuli a human can detect in its finger skin. Mechanical contact can be detected at small applied forces due to the high sensitivity of the membrane-based taxels to deformations, replicating Meissner endings and Merkel endings [75]. The function of Pacinian endings to sense vibration can be registered by the same taxels by sampling them at high enough speed as shown in Fig. 3.8. This allows the detection of slippage and surface roughness as visible in Fig. 4.13 as well as feature extraction with neural networks discussed in section 4.6.2. The capability of Ruffini endings to measure strain or tangential forces is possible by adding three electrodes in some of the taxels, giving directional force information. Temperature sensing is another important sense for our capabilities of safe interaction and surface classification. The integration of resistive temperature sensing structures in the flexible substrate is possible, was however not evaluated in detail. Combining those functionalities with the 0.5 mm cell size of the taxels and the possibility to fully integrate them in soft material results in a promising approach for a replication of the human sense of touch.

6.1.2 Commercial potential

The main field of application of the developed technology focuses on sensing of tactile information on relatively small, possibly soft, surfaces. The technology is less competitive in large area sensing as the fabrication costs mainly depend on the area. Several sensing technologies fabricated in the meso- and macroscale might be more cost-efficient.

Table 6.2 summarizes possible applications and the key markets, the list is not exhaustive. Product requirements like robustness, biological compatibility or sensitivities will strongly depend on the chosen application.

Table 6.2: Application and market overview.

Application	Markets
Sensitive grippers	Warehouse robotics
	Collaborative robotics
	Personal assistance robotics
	Medical robotics / Teleoperation
	Trash sorting robots
	Hazard support robots
	Harvesting / animal care robots
Sensitive skin	Prostheses
Sensing surface on small bodies	Medical devices / Catheters
	Controllers, touch pads

6.2 Outlook

Not all challenges could be solved. Most integration tasks are merely open engineering packages, there are however three major fields of future work which need further research:

1. Feature extraction with neural networks: Most advanced tactile sensing technologies use neural networks for feature extraction [18, 21, 76]. This allows better abstraction of information from the rich sensor data. Such data-driven approaches show higher robustness to existing measurement imperfections (viscoelastic effects and sensor response variations). We initiated work in this field (see section 4.6), there are however still many open questions.

2. Robotic integration: Closed-loop applications in a robotic gripper

would ultimately give feedback on how to optimize the finger topology, suggesting ideal skin thickness and the positioning of the taxels as well as necessary data rates of individual taxels. Such applications would greatly benefit from integrated circuits for the readout and pre-processing of sensor information. This would allow a much smaller footprint, the readout of larger taxels arrays and the compression of sensor information before the data transfer to a central processing unit.

3. Robustness: Further robustness studies are necessary to prove the applicability of the technology. They however would need to be clearly defined, as applicable loads will strongly depend on the use case. There are multiple approaches to improve the robustness, which could however not be investigated for timely reasons.

A List of samples

A.1 List of cleanroom samples

Table A.1 explains the sample description code, which was used over the course of the thesis. Each sample in each fabrication step was classified by its shape (first number) and a code of exposed surface materials (letters with numbers). Two example codes are:

1. 1-A1: 100 mm wafer with Si surface

2. 11-C1B1B3: 20 mm chip with PI & Ti - Au surface

Table A.1: Sample description code

Size code	Description	Material Code	Exposed surface material
0	Random substrate shape	A1	Si
1	100mm wafer	A2	Glass
		A3	SiO2
11	Chip (<=20mm)	B1	Ti
12	Chip (>20mm)	B2	Cu
		B3	Au
21	Chip on Carrier (specify both materials)	B4	InSn
		B5	Al
		C1	Polyimide
		C2	Photoresist
		C3	Sacrificial Polymer (LOR)

The fabricated substrates are summarized in Table A.3. Only complete wafers of GEN1 and higher are displayed to shorten the overall list. The samples used in each publication are listed with the following code: 1 = [1]; 2 = [47]; 3 = [2]. The naming convention of devices and taxels is described in Table A.2.

Table A.2: Naming convention of devices and taxels is $Ax\_y\_Dz\_mSn$ with the following parameters:

Variable	Description	Explanation
x	Wafer number	From Table A.3
y	Device number	1-5, compare Figs. 2.11 & 2.13
z	Device type	D1 - D3 for GEN2, DL or DR for GEN3. compare Figs. 2.11 & 2.13
m,n	Taxel index	Fig. 2.4

A.2 List of fingers

Table A.4 summarizes all fabricated fingers including the chosen finger design and used cleanroom devices (array ID).

Table A.3: List of substrates

General				Purpose	
Action	Sample ID	Substrate desc.	Date	Mask Gen	In public.
Membrane integration tests	A80	11-A1	05.08.19	Gen1	
Membrane integration tests	A81	11-A1	05.08.19	Gen1	
Process Test on Chip level	A105	1-A1	17.10.19	Gen1	
Process Test on Chip level	A106	1-A1	17.10.19	Gen1	
Process Test on Chip level	A111	1-A1	7.11.19	Gen1	
Process Test on Chip level	A112	1-A1	7.11.19	Gen1	
Process Test on Chip level	A116	1-A1	19.11.19	Gen1	
Process Test on Chip level	A117	1-A1	19.11.19	Gen1	
Full fab substrate	A118	1-A1	19.11.19	Gen2	
Full fab substrate	A119	1-A1	19.11.19	Gen2	
Full fab substrate	A120	1-A1	19.11.19	Gen2	
Process Test on Chip level	A123	1-A1	20.12.19	Gen1	
Process Test on Chip level	A124	1-A1	20.12.19	Gen1	
Process Test on Chip level	A129	1-A1	31.01.20	Gen1	
Full fab substrate	A130	1-A1	18.2.20	Gen2	
Full fab substrate	A131	1-A1	18.2.20	Gen2	
Full fab substrate	A132	1-A1	18.2.20	Gen2	
Full fab substrate	A133	1-A1	18.2.20	Gen2	
Full fab substrate	A134	1-A1	18.2.20	Gen2	
Full fab substrate	A135	1-A1	18.2.20	Gen2	
Full fab substrate	A136	1-A1	18.2.20	Gen2	
Full fab substrate	A147	1-A1	16.3.20	Gen2	
Full fab substrate	A148	1-A1	16.3.20	Gen2	
Full fab substrate	A149	1-A1	16.3.20	Gen2	
Full fab substrate	A150	1-A1	16.3.20	Gen2	
Flex substrate optimizations	A157	1-A1	18.5.20	Gen2	
Flex substrate optimizations	A158	1-A1	18.5.20	Gen2	
Flex substrate optimizations	A159	1-A1	18.5.20	Gen2	
Flex substrate optimizations	A160	1-A1	18.5.20	Gen2	
Flex substrate optimizations	A161	1-A1	18.5.20	Gen2	
Flex substrate optimizations	A162	1-A1	26.5.20	Gen2	
Flex substrate optimizations	A163	1-A1	26.5.20	Gen2	
Flex substrate optimizations	A164	1-A1	26.5.20	Gen2	
Flex substrate optimizations	A165	1-A1	2.6.20	Gen2	
Flex substrate optimizations	A166	1-A1	2.6.20	Gen2	
Flex substrate optimizations	A167	1-A1	2.6.20	Gen2	
Flex substrate optimizations	A168	1-A1	2.6.20	Gen2	
Full fab substrate	A169	1-A1	11.6.20	Gen2	
Full fab substrate	A170	1-A1	11.6.20	Gen2	
Full fab substrate	A171	1-A1	11.6.20	Gen2	
Full fab substrate	A172	1-A1	11.6.20	Gen2	
Full fab substrate	A173	1-A1	11.6.20	Gen2	
Full fab substrate	A179	1-A1	30.6.20	Gen2	
Full fab substrate	A180	1-A1	30.6.20	Gen2	
Full fab substrate	A181	1-A1	30.6.20	Gen2	
Full fab substrate	A182	1-A1	30.6.20	Gen2	
Full fab substrate	A183	1-A1	14.7.20	Gen2	
Full fab substrate	A184	1-A1	14.7.20	Gen2	
Full fab substrate	A185	1-A1	14.7.20	Gen2	
Full fab substrate	A186	1-A1	22.09.20	Gen2	
Full fab substrate	A187	1-A1	22.09.20	Gen2	
Full fab substrate	A188	1-A1	22.09.20	Gen2	
Full fab substrate	A189	1-A1	22.09.20	Gen2	
Full fab substrate	A194	1-A1	27.8.20	Gen2	1
Full fab substrate	A195	1-A1	27.8.20	Gen2	1
Full fab substrate	A196	1-A1	27.8.20	Gen2	1
Full fab substrate	A197	1-A1	27.8.20	Gen2	1
Full fab substrate	A200	1-A1	11.9.20	Gen2	
Full fab substrate	A201	1-A1	11.9.20	Gen2	

General				Purpose	
Action	Sample ID	Substrate desc.	Date	Mask Gen	In public.
Full fab substrate	A202	1-A1	11.9.20	Gen2	
Full fab substrate	A203	1-A1	11.9.20	Gen2	
Full fab substrate	A204	1-A1	26.10.20	Gen2	2
Full fab substrate	A205	1-A1	26.10.20	Gen2	
Full fab substrate	A206	1-A1	26.10.20	Gen2	3
Full fab substrate	A207	1-A1	26.10.20	Gen2	
Full fab substrate	A214	1-A1	12.2.21	Gen2	
Full fab substrate	A215	1-A1	12.2.21	Gen2	
Full fab substrate	A216	1-A1	12.2.21	Gen2	
Full fab substrate	A217	1-A1	12.2.21	Gen2	
Full fab substrate	A240	1-A1	01.09.21	Gen3	3
Full fab substrate	A241	1-A1	01.09.21	Gen3	3
Full fab substrate	A242	1-A1	01.09.21	Gen3	3
Full fab substrate	A243	1-A1	01.09.21	Gen3	3
Full fab substrate	A277	1-A1	08.12.21	Gen3	
Full fab substrate	A278	1-A1	08.12.21	Gen3	
Full fab substrate	A279	1-A1	08.12.21	Gen3	
Full fab substrate	A280	1-A1	08.12.21	Gen3	
Full fab substrate	A283	1-A1	16.12.21	Gen3	
Full fab substrate	A284	1-A1	16.12.21	Gen3	
Full fab substrate	A285	1-A1	16.12.21	Gen3	
Full fab substrate	A286	1-A1	16.12.21	Gen3	
Full fab substrate	A287	1-A1	08.02.22	Gen3	
Full fab substrate	A288	1-A1	08.02.22	Gen3	3
Full fab substrate	A289	1-A1	08.02.22	Gen3	
Full fab substrate	A290	1-A1	08.02.22	Gen3	
Full fab substrate	A300	1-A1	14.6.22	Gen3	
Full fab substrate	A301	1-A1	14.6.22	Gen3	
Full fab substrate	A302	1-A1	14.6.22	Gen3	
Full fab substrate	A303	1-A1	14.6.22	Gen3	
Full fab substrate	A304	1-A1	12.7.22	Gen3	
Full fab substrate	A305	1-A1	12.7.22	Gen3	
Full fab substrate	A306	1-A1	12.7.22	Gen3	
Full fab substrate	A307	1-A1	12.7.22	Gen3	3
Full fab substrate	A308	1-A1	24.8.22	Gen3	
Full fab substrate	A309	1-A1	24.8.22	Gen3	
Full fab substrate	A310	1-A1	24.8.22	Gen3	
Full fab substrate	A311	1-A1	24.8.22	Gen3	
Full fab substrate	A312	1-A1	25.8.22	Gen3	
Full fab substrate	A313	1-A1	25.8.22	Gen3	
Full fab substrate	A314	1-A1	25.8.22	Gen3	
Full fab substrate	A315	1-A1	25.8.22	Gen3	
Full fab substrate	A318	1-A1	10.10.22	Gen3	
Full fab substrate	A319	1-A1	10.10.22	Gen3	
Full fab substrate	A320	1-A1	10.10.22	Gen3	
Full fab substrate	A321	1-A1	10.10.22	Gen3	
Full fab substrate	A322	1-A1	10.10.22	Gen3	
Full fab substrate	A323	1-A1	10.10.22	Gen3	
Full fab substrate	A324	1-A1	10.10.22	Gen3	
Full fab substrate	A325	1-A1	10.10.22	Gen3	
Full fab substrate	A326	1-A1	11.10.22	Gen3	
Full fab substrate	A327	1-A1	11.10.22	Gen3	
Full fab substrate	A328	1-A1	11.10.22	Gen3	
Full fab substrate	A329	1-A1	11.10.22	Gen3	
Full fab substrate	A330	1-A1	30.11.22	Gen3	
Full fab substrate	A331	1-A1	30.11.22	Gen3	
Full fab substrate	A332	1-A1	30.11.22	Gen3	
Full fab substrate	A333	1-A1	30.11.22	Gen3	

Table A.4: List of artificial fingers.

General			Date	Array ID
Action	ID	Finger design	Date	Array ID
Test Finger integration	F1	V1	19.9.21	A186
Finger with sensing array	F2	V2_2.5mm	2.3.22	A242-2-DL
Finger with sensing array	F3	V2_2.5mm	8.3.22	A242-2-DR
Finger with sensing array	F4	V3_3.3mm	4.4.22	A242-3-DR
Finger with sensing array	F5	V3_3.3mm	12.4.22	A242-4-DR
Finger with sensing array	F6	V3_3.3mm	29.4.22	A278-2-DL
Finger with sensing array	F7	V3_3.3mm	29.4.22	A242-1-DR
Finger with sensing array	F8	V3_3.3mm	24.5.22	A242-5-DR
Finger with sensing array	F9	V3_3.3mm	21.6.22	A283-2-DL
Finger with sensing array	F10	V3_3.3mm	5.7.22	A284-2-DL
Finger with sensing array	F11	V3_3.3mm	6.7.22	A284-3-DL
Finger with sensing array	F12	V3_3.3mm	8.7.22	A284-5-DL
Finger with sensing array	F13	V3_3.3mm	14.7.22	A288-3-DL
Finger with sensing array	F14	V3_3.3mm	15.7.22	A288-3-DR
Finger with sensing array	F15	V3_3.3mm	18.7.22	A288-5-DL
Finger with sensing array	F16	V3_3.3mm	19.7.22	A288-5-DR
Finger with sensing array	F17	V3_3.3mm	21.7.22	A288-1-DL
Finger with sensing array	F18	V3_3.3mm	12.8.22	A289-3-DL
Finger with sensing array	F19	V3_3.3mm	16.8.22	A289-5-DL
Finger with sensing array	F20	V3_3.3mm	18.8.22	A289-5-DR
Finger with sensing array	F21	V3_3.3mm	7.10.22	A302-5-DR
Finger with sensing array	F22	V3_3.3mm	14.10.22	A306-2-DR
Finger with sensing array	F23	V3_3.3mm	28.10.22	A307-2-DL
Finger with sensing array	F24	V3_3.3mm	1.11.22	A307-3-DL
Finger with sensing array	F25	V3_3.3mm	8.11.22	A307-4-DR
Finger with sensing array	F26	V3_3.3mm	14.11.22	A309-2-DL
Finger with sensing array	F27	V3_3.3mm	18.11.22	A309-3-DL
Finger with sensing array	F28	V3_3.3mm	18.11.22	A309-3-DR
Finger with sensing array	F29	V3_3.3mm	18.11.22	A311-2-DR
Finger with sensing array	F30	V3_3.3mm	21.11.22	A311-3-DR
Finger with sensing array	F31	V3_3.3mm	22.11.22	A311-3-DL
Finger with sensing array	F32	V3_3.3mm	7.12.22	A312-5-DL
Finger with sensing array	F33	V3_3.3mm	16.1.23	A313-2-DL

B Additional information on setups & materials

B.1 Characterization setup

This section holds some additional information for the characterization setup. Fig. B.1 shows which sensors are connected to which contact pads in GEN2 devices. This information was important in the experiments with EV0. All newer sensor-to-MUX conversions are directly implemented in the driver scripts of either the AD2 (EV1) or the Eclypse Z7 readout (EV2 & EV3). They can be found in the Python initialization routines.

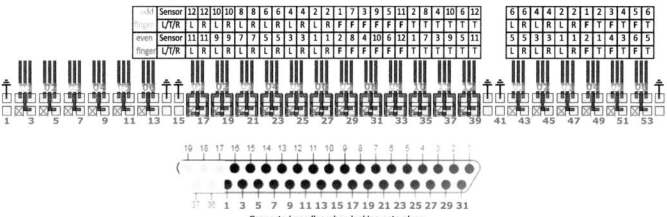

Figure B.1: Contact pads in GEN2 devices.

Fig. B.2 shows how one of the settings tabs is set up. The parameter lists are generated dynamically in the code and can therefore be easily adapted to new variables in functions.

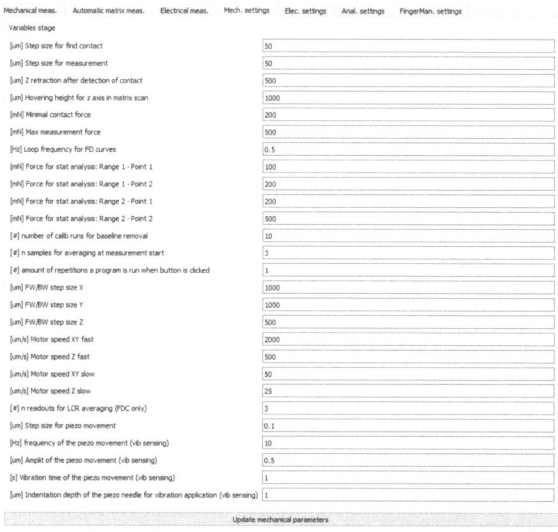

Mechanical meas.	Automatic matrix meas.	Electrical meas.	Mech. settings	Elec. settings	Anal. settings	FingerMan. settings

Variables stage

[um] Step size for find contact	50
[um] Step size for measurement	50
[um] Z retraction after detection of contact	500
[um] Hovering height for z axis in matrix scan	1000
[mN] Minimal contact force	200
[mN] Max measurement force	500
[Hz] Loop frequency for FD curves	0.5
[mN] Force for stat analysis: Range 1 - Point 1	100
[mN] Force for stat analysis: Range 1 - Point 2	200
[mN] Force for stat analysis: Range 2 - Point 1	200
[mN] Force for stat analysis: Range 2 - Point 2	500
[#] number of calib runs for baseline removal	10
[#] n samples for averaging at measurement start	3
[#] amount of repetitions a program is run when button is clicked	1
[um] FW/BW step size X	1000
[um] FW/BW step size Y	1000
[um] FW/BW step size Z	500
[um/s] Motor speed XY fast	2000
[um/s] Motor speed Z fast	500
[um/s] Motor speed XY slow	50
[um/s] Motor speed Z slow	25
[#] n readouts for LCR averaging (FDC only)	3
[um] Step size for piezo movement	0.1
[Hz] frequency of the piezo movement (vib sensing)	10
[um] Amplit of the piezo movement (vib sensing)	0.5
[s] Vibration time of the piezo movement (vib sensing)	1
[um] Indentation depth of the piezo needle for vibration application (vib sensing)	1

Update mechanical parameters

Figure B.2: Mechanical settings tab allowing the configuration of measurements

The fluctuation issues, which are shown in Fig. 5.11b and disturbed the endurance tests in [1] could be reduced by using a network stabilizer as shown in Fig. B.3.

Figure B.3: Network stabilizer

B.2 Material overview

Table B.1: Summary of material properties. Data is based on web sources (MatWeb, AZOM), data sheets of suppliers and partially on self-performed measurements. Used materials are highlighted in green.

			Substrate		Metallization					Carrier polymer							Encapsulation material			
	Properties	Unit	Si	Glass (Borofloat 3.3)	Ti	Cu	Cr	Ni	Au	PI 2611	PI 5878G	PI Durimide 7300	Mylar (Polyester)	Polyurethane	SU-8 (Epoxies)	Parylene C	PDMS-Nusil Med 4905	PDMS-Sylgard 182	PDMS-Dragonskin 10	PDMS-Dragonskin 20
Mechanical	Young's Modulus	[GPa]			116	110	140		209	8.5	2.3	2.5	5	0.008-0.8		2.8	2.40E-03	0.002	2.80E-04	4.95E-04
	Yield strength	[MPa]			140	33.3			59				100			55	2.4		2.75	3.79
	Elastic strain	[%]			0.12	0.03	0.03		0.03							3				
	Tensile strength	[MPa]			220	210	282		317	350	260	215	210	1.65		65		6.7		
	Maximum strain	[%]			54	60			30	100	120	85	100	>14		200	1000	100-200	663	620
	Poisson's Ratio	[]			0.34	0.343	0.31	0.31	0.31											
	Density	[g/cm^3]			4.5	8.93	7.19	8.88		1.4	1.42		1.39			1.29			1.07	1.08
	Film stress (only guideline)	[MPa]			-400 -700		200 900-1400	200-300	200	2	16									
	Hardness Type A																7		10	20
Thermal	Melting point	[°C]			1650	1083	1907	1455		360	400	285		170		290				
	CTE	[1/1e6 K]	2.6	3.3	8.9	16.4	6.2	13.1		3	20	55	17	100-200		35	340			
	Thermal conductivity	[W/mK]			17	385	69.1	60.7		0.1	0.15			0.11		0.08		0.27		
Electrical	Resistivity	[Ohm m]			5.54E-07	1.70E-08	1.30E-07	6.40E-08		1.00E+16	1.00E+21					8.80E+18		2.90E+14		
	Dielectric Breakdown	[V/m]			N/A	N/A	N/A	N/A		2.00E+08	2.00E+08		2.70E+08					1.90E+07		
	Dielectric constant [1kHz]				N/A	N/A	N/A	N/A		2.9	3.15	3.2	3.2			3.1		2.7		
	Dissipation factor [1kHz]				N/A	N/A	N/A	N/A		0.002	0.002		0.005			0.019		0.002		
Vacu um	Moisture uptake	[%]			N/A	N/A	N/A	N/A		0.5	2.5	1.08	0.6-0.8			0.06		0.002		
	Weight loss	[%]			N/A	N/A	N/A	N/A		1	3.6							High		
Processing	Processing		Possible use as carrier material							No photo patterning	Photopatternable		Only as foil available		Brittle (initial experiment)	Conformal coating				

133

C Supplementary data

C.1 Artificial finger - Touch and Slide

This section summarizes the supporting information for the Touch and Slide experiments on F14. Movie `https://youtu.be/z8JW3mJ76uo` shows the camera footage and the pressure & X/Y arrow plots for the movement of the stamp into the three directions -X, Y & -Y. Fig. C.1 shows the measurement data for the touch and slide experiment in -Y direction, analog to the data displayed in Fig. 4.12.

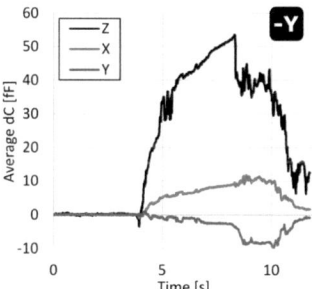

Figure C.1: Averages of all taxel capacitances for the touch & slide experiment in -Y direction.

C.2 Artificial finger - Robustness tests

An initial robustness study was performed on F24 for publication. Fig. C.2 displays the results, which are comparable with the studies presented in Fig. 4.15. A few additional observations are summarized here, which are also applicable to the studies presented in the main text:

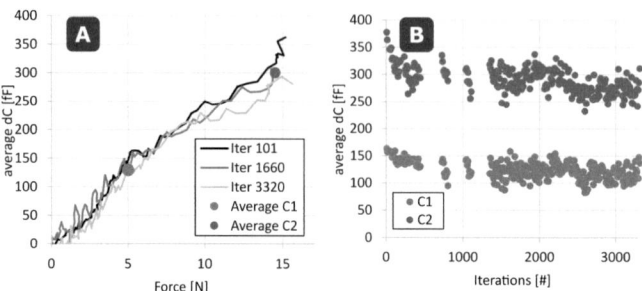

Figure C.2: Robustness tests on F24: Average of all sensor capacitances for applying forces in the range of 0 - 15 N for >3000 iterations. [2]

- Movie https://youtu.be/SGydWnM92mk shows a video of the robustness testing routine, displaying the deformation of the finger under higher load.

- All plots have a discontinuity at around 14-15 N, which origins from a discontinuity of the applied force during the downwards movement of the stamp. This behavior depends on the deformation of the finger bulk and was observed for all tested fingers. The FD curve is shown in Fig. C.3.

- The gaps in the measurement series in Fig. C.2 originate from data logging issues after the readout went into an error state. The error state arose from the Z-stage motor, which has a maximum force range of 20 N. In the first 1300 measurement iterations, a relatively large step size was chosen, which sometimes resulted in a force excessing the 20 N range. The problem was fixed by changing to a finer step size, after which 2 x 1000 iterations ran without further issues. This method was also used for the testing of all other fingers.

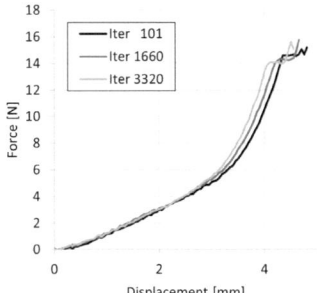

Figure C.3: Force-Displacement plots of F24 in the endurance tests: showing a discontinuity at around 14-15N

F26 was used for some additional studies before and after the endurance test. Fig. C.4 shows the reaction of F26 to the rough stamp, which is comparable with the data presented for the smooth stamp in Fig. 4.17. An additional experiment after the endurance test tested the behavior of an oiled versus a dry stamp. Fig. C.5 shows the different finger responses, which are discussed in the main text.

137

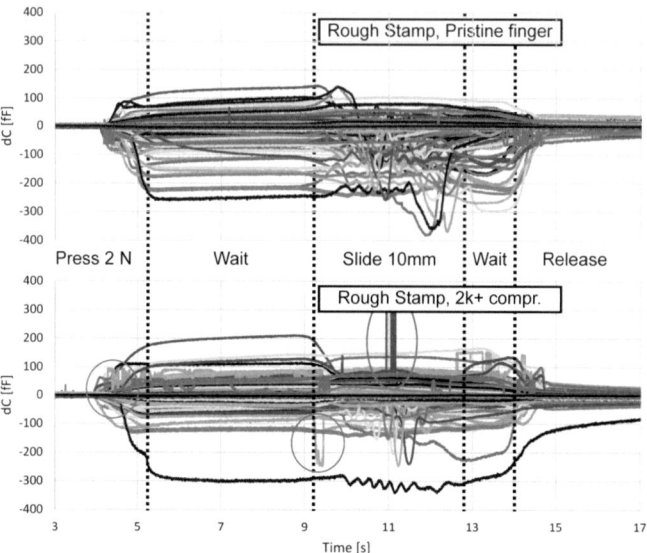

Figure C.4: Touch & Slide (-X) experiment on F26 (stabilized membrane) before and after an endurance test (2k+ compressions) with the rough stamp.

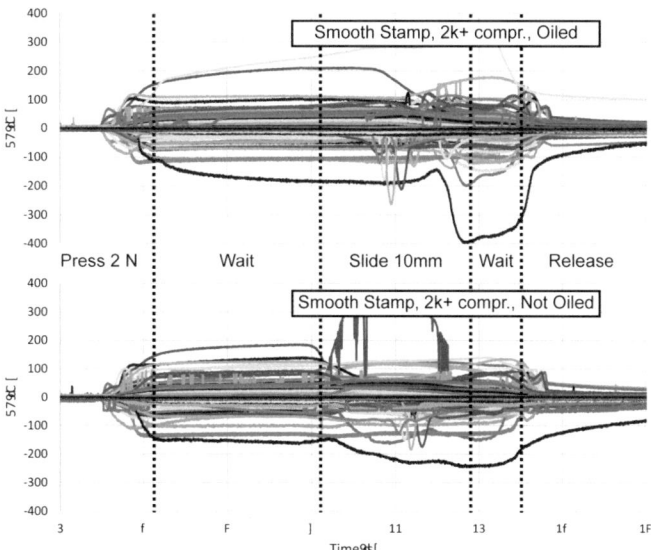

Figure C.5: Finger readout (F26) while sliding (-X) a smooth stamp after the endurance test (2k+ compressions). The surface is either oiled with silicone oil (top) or not (bottom).

Bibliography

[1] J. Weichart, C. Roman, and C. Hierold, "Tactile Sensing With Scalable Capacitive Sensor Arrays on Flexible Substrates," *Journal of Microelectromechanical Systems*, vol. 30, no. 6, pp. 915–929, 2021, DOI: http://dx.doi.org/10.1109/JMEMS.2021.3104352.

[2] J. Weichart, P. Sivananthaguru, F. B. Coulter, T. Burger, and C. Hierold, "Artificial fingertip with high resolution tactile sensing capabilities," *Submitted to: Soft robotics*, 2023.

[3] A. Billard and D. Kragic, "Trends and challenges in robot manipulation," *Science*, vol. 364, no. 6446, 2019, DOI: http://dx.doi.org/10.1126/science.aat8414.

[4] L. D. Harmon, "Automated Tactile Sensing," *The International Journal of Robotics Research*, pp. 3–32, 1982.

[5] J. A. George, D. T. Kluger, T. S. Davis, S. M. Wendelken, E. V. Okorokova, Q. He, C. C. Duncan, D. T. Hutchinson, Z. C. Thumser, D. T. Beckler, P. D. Marasco, S. J. Bensmaia, and G. A. Clark, "Biomimetic sensory feedback through peripheral nerve stimulation improves dexterous use of a bionic hand," *Science Robotics*, vol. 4, no. 32, pp. 1–12, 2019, DOI: http://dx.doi.org/10.1126/scirobotics.aax2352.

[6] R. S. Johansson and J. R. Flanagan, "Coding and use of tactile signals from the fingertips in object manipulation tasks," *Nature Reviews Neuroscience*, vol. 10, no. 5, pp. 345–359, 2009, DOI: http://dx.doi.org/10.1038/nrn2621.

[7] R. S. Dahiya, G. Metta, M. Valle, and G. Sandini, "Tactile sensing-from humans to humanoids," *IEEE Transactions on Robotics*, vol. 26, no. 1, pp. 1–20, 2010, DOI: http://dx.doi.org/10.1109/TRO.2009.2033627.

[8] E. S. Dellon, R. Mourey, A. L. Dellon, and A. L. Dellon, "Human Pressure Perception Values for Constant and Moving One- and Two-Point Discrimination," *Plastic and Reconstructive Surgery*, vol. 90, no. 1, 1992.

[9] C. M. Boutry, M. Jorda, O. Vardoulis, O. Khatib, Z. Bao, M. Negre, and A. Chortos, "A hierarchically patterned, bioinspired e-skin able to detect the direction of applied pressure for robotics," *Science Robotics*, vol. 3, no. 24, p. eaau6914, 2018, DOI: http://dx.doi.org/10.1126/scirobotics.aau6914.

[10] S. J. Xie, Y. Lu, S. Yoon, J. Yang, and D. S. Park, "Intensity variation normalization for finger vein recognition using guided filter based singe scale retinex," *Sensors (Switzerland)*, vol. 15, no. 7, pp. 17 089–17 105, 2015, DOI: http://dx.doi.org/10.3390/s150717089.

[11] S. A. Darby and R. J. Frysztak, "Neuroanatomy of the spinal cord," *Clinical Anatomy of the Spine, Spinal Cord, and ANS*, pp. 341–412, 2014.

[12] H. Yousef, M. Boukallel, and K. Althoefer, "Tactile sensing for dexterous in-hand manipulation in robotics - A review," *Sensors and Actuators, A: Physical*, vol. 167, no. 2, pp. 171–187, 2011, DOI: http://dx.doi.org/10.1016/j.sna.2011.02.038.

[13] L. Zou, C. Ge, Z. J. Wang, E. Cretu, and X. Li, "Novel tactile sensor technology and smart tactile sensing systems: A review," *Sensors (Switzerland)*, vol. 17, no. 11, pp. 1–24, 2017, DOI: http://dx.doi.org/10.3390/s17112653.

[14] M. Park, B.-G. Bok, J.-H. Ahn, and M.-S. Kim, "Recent Advances in Tactile Sensing Technology," *Micromachines*, vol. 9, no. 7, p. 321, jun 2018, DOI: http://dx.doi.org/10.3390/mi9070321.

[15] J. A. Fishel and G. E. Loeb, "Bayesian exploration for intelligent identification of textures," *Frontiers in Neurorobotics*, vol. 6, pp. 1–20, 2012, DOI: http://dx.doi.org/10.3389/fnbot.2012.00004.

[16] F. Veiga, R. Akrour, and J. Peters, "Hierarchical Tactile-Based Control Decomposition of Dexterous In-Hand Manipulation Tasks," *Frontiers in Robotics and AI*, vol. 7, no. November, pp. 1–12, 2020, DOI: http://dx.doi.org/10.3389/frobt.2020.521448.

[17] M. Lambeta, P. W. Chou, S. Tian, B. Yang, B. Maloon, V. R. Most, D. Stroud, R. Santos, A. Byagowi, G. Kammerer, D. Jayaraman, and R. Calandra, "DIGIT: A Novel Design for a Low-Cost Compact High-Resolution Tactile Sensor with Application to In-Hand Manipulation," *IEEE Robotics and Automation Letters*, vol. 5, no. 3, pp. 3838–3845, 2020, DOI: http://dx.doi.org/10.1109/LRA.2020.2977257.

142

[18] W. Yuan, S. Dong, and E. H. Adelson, "GelSight: High-resolution robot tactile sensors for estimating geometry and force," *Sensors (Switzerland)*, vol. 17, no. 12, 2017, DOI: http://dx.doi.org/10.3390/s17122762.

[19] A. Padmanabha, F. Ebert, S. Tian, R. Calandra, C. Finn, and S. Levine, "OmniTact: A Multi-Directional High-Resolution Touch Sensor," *Proceedings - IEEE International Conference on Robotics and Automation*, pp. 618–624, 2020, DOI: http://dx.doi.org/10.1109/ICRA40945.2020.9196712.

[20] C. Sferrazza and R. D'Andrea, "Sim-to-Real for High-Resolution Optical Tactile Sensing: From Images to Three-Dimensional Contact Force Distributions," *Soft robotics*, vol. 9, no. 5, pp. 926–937, 2022, DOI: http://dx.doi.org/10.1089/soro.2020.0213.

[21] H. Sun, K. J. Kuchenbecker, and G. Martius, "A soft thumb-sized vision-based sensor with accurate all-round force perception," *Nature Machine Intelligence*, vol. 4, no. 2, pp. 135–145, 2022, DOI: http://dx.doi.org/10.1038/s42256-021-00439-3.

[22] T. P. Tomo, A. Schmitz, W. K. Wong, H. Kristanto, S. Somlor, J. Hwang, L. Jamone, and S. Sugano, "Covering a Robot Fingertip with uSkin: A Soft Electronic Skin with Distributed 3-Axis Force Sensitive Elements for Robot Hands," *IEEE Robotics and Automation Letters*, vol. 3, no. 1, pp. 124–131, 2018, DOI: http://dx.doi.org/10.1109/LRA.2017.2734965.

[23] A. Mohammadi, Y. Xu, Y. Tan, P. Choong, and D. Oetomo, "Magnetic-based soft tactile sensors with deformable continuous force transfer medium for resolving contact locations in robotic grasping and manipulation," *Sensors (Switzerland)*, vol. 19, no. 22, pp. 1–14, 2019, DOI: http://dx.doi.org/10.3390/s19224925.

[24] R. Bhirangi, T. Hellebrekers, C. Majidi, and A. Gupta, "ReSkin: versatile, replaceable, lasting tactile skins," in *Conference on Robot Learning*, 2022, pp. 587–597.

[25] A. Drimus, G. Kootstra, A. Bilberg, and D. Kragic, "Design of a flexible tactile sensor for classification of rigid and deformable objects," *Robotics and Autonomous Systems*, vol. 62, no. 1, pp. 3–15, 2014, DOI: http://dx.doi.org/10.1016/j.robot.2012.07.021.

[26] G. H. Büscher, R. Kõiva, C. Schürmann, R. Haschke, and H. J. Ritter, "Flexible and stretchable fabric-based tactile sensor," *Robotics*

and Autonomous Systems, vol. 63, no. P3, pp. 244–252, jan 2015, DOI: http://dx.doi.org/10.1016/j.robot.2014.09.007.

[27] M. Teyssier, G. Bailly, C. Pelachaud, E. Lecolinet, A. Conn, and A. Roudaut, "Skin-on interfaces: A bio-driven approach for artificial skin design to cover interactive devices," *UIST 2019 - Proceedings of the 32nd Annual ACM Symposium on User Interface Software and Technology*, pp. 307–322, 2019, DOI: http://dx.doi.org/10.1145/3332165. 3347943.

[28] H. Oh, G. C. Yi, M. Yip, and S. A. Dayeh, "Supplementary - Scalable tactile sensor arrays on flexible substrates with high spatiotemporal resolution enabling slip and grip for closed-loop robotics," *Science Advances*, vol. 6, no. 46, 2020, DOI: http://dx.doi.org/10.1126/sciadv. abd7795.

[29] H. K. Lee, J. Chung, S. I. Chang, and E. Yoon, "Normal and shear force measurement using a flexible polymer tactile sensor with embedded multiple capacitors," *Journal of Microelectromechanical Systems*, vol. 17, no. 4, pp. 934–942, 2008, DOI: http://dx.doi.org/10.1109/ JMEMS.2008.921727.

[30] G. Liang, Y. Wang, D. Mei, K. Xi, and Z. Chen, "Flexible Capacitive Tactile Sensor Array With Truncated Pyramids as Dielectric Layer for Three-Axis Force Measurement," *J. Microelectromechanical Syst.*, vol. 24, no. 5, pp. 1–10, 2015, DOI: http://dx.doi.org/10.1109/JMEMS. 2015.2418095.

[31] S. Chun, W. Son, H. Kim, S. K. Lim, C. Pang, and C. Choi, "Self-Powered Pressure- and Vibration-Sensitive Tactile Sensors for Learning Technique-Based Neural Finger Skin," *Nano Letters*, vol. 19, no. 5, pp. 3305–3312, may 2019, DOI: http://dx.doi.org/10.1021/acs. nanolett.9b00922.

[32] T. Someya, Y. Kato, T. Sakurai, T. Sekitani, H. Kawaguchi, and S. Iba, "A large-area, flexible pressure sensor matrix with organic field-effect transistors for artificial skin applications," *Proceedings of the National Academy of Sciences*, vol. 101, no. 27, pp. 9966–9970, 2004, DOI: http: //dx.doi.org/10.1073/pnas.0401918101.

[33] D. Zhu, D. Huang, F. Zhang, Y. Zang, C.-a. Di, and X. Gao, "Flexible suspended gate organic thin-film transistors for ultra-sensitive pressure detection," *Nature Communications*, vol. 6, no. 1, pp. 1–9, 2015, DOI: http://dx.doi.org/10.1038/ncomms7269.

[34] A. Schmitz, P. Maiolino, M. Maggiali, L. Natale, G. Cannata, and G. Metta, "Methods and technologies for the implementation of large-scale robot tactile sensors," *IEEE Transactions on Robotics*, vol. 27, no. 3, pp. 389–400, 2011, DOI: http://dx.doi.org/10.1109/TRO.2011.2132930.

[35] J. A. Rogers, T. Someya, and Y. Huang, "Materials and mechanics for stretchable electronics," *Science*, vol. 327, no. 5973, pp. 1603–1607, 2010, DOI: http://dx.doi.org/10.1126/science.1182383.

[36] J. Weichart, C. Roman, and C. Hierold, "Sensor System for a three-dimensional device, European Patent EP4067849," 2021.

[37] K. Tybrandt, D. Khodagholy, B. Dielacher, F. Stauffer, A. F. Renz, G. Buzsáki, and J. Vörös, "High-Density Stretchable Electrode Grids for Chronic Neural Recording," *Advanced Materials*, vol. 30, no. 15, 2018, DOI: http://dx.doi.org/10.1002/adma.201706520.

[38] I. M. Graz, D. P. Cotton, and S. P. Lacour, "Extended cyclic uniaxial loading of stretchable gold thin-films on elastomeric substrates," *Applied Physics Letters*, vol. 94, no. 7, 2009, DOI: http://dx.doi.org/10.1063/1.3076103.

[39] N. Lu, Z. Suo, and J. J. Vlassak, "The effect of film thickness on the failure strain of polymer-supported metal films," *Acta Materialia*, vol. 58, no. 5, pp. 1679–1687, 2010, DOI: http://dx.doi.org/10.1016/j.actamat.2009.11.010.

[40] J. Sun, Q. Hua, C. Pan, Z. L. Wang, H. Liu, R. Yu, R. Bao, and J. Zhai, "Skin-inspired highly stretchable and conformable matrix networks for multifunctional sensing," *Nature Communications*, vol. 9, no. 1, pp. 1–11, 2018, DOI: http://dx.doi.org/10.1038/s41467-017-02685-9.

[41] M. Jablonski, R. Lucchini, F. Bossuyt, T. Vervust, J. Vanfleteren, J. W. De Vries, P. Vena, and M. Gonzalez, "Impact of geometry on stretchable meandered interconnect uniaxial tensile extension fatigue reliability," *Microelectronics Reliability*, vol. 55, no. 1, pp. 143–154, 2015, DOI: http://dx.doi.org/10.1016/j.microrel.2014.09.009.

[42] K. Kim, K. R. Lee, W. H. Kim, K. B. Park, T. H. Kim, J. S. Kim, and J. J. Pak, "Polymer-based flexible tactile sensor up to 32 x 32 arrays integrated with interconnection terminals," *Sensors and Actuators, A: Physical*, vol. 156, no. 2, pp. 284–291, 2009, DOI: http://dx.doi.org/10.1016/j.sna.2009.08.015.

[43] H.-j. K. J.-h. K. W.-c. Choi, "Development of a flexible three-axial tactile sensor array for a robotic finger," *Microsyst Technol.*, pp. 1721–1726, 2011, DOI: http://dx.doi.org/10.1007/s00542-011-1368-x.

[44] D. P. Cotton, P. H. Chappell, A. Cranny, N. M. White, and S. P. Beeby, "A novel thick-film piezoelectric slip sensor for a prosthetic hand," *IEEE Sensors Journal*, vol. 7, no. 5, pp. 752–761, 2007, DOI: http://dx.doi.org/10.1109/JSEN.2007.894912.

[45] R. L. Truby, M. Wehner, A. K. Grosskopf, D. M. Vogt, S. G. Uzel, R. J. Wood, and J. A. Lewis, "Soft Somatosensitive Actuators via Embedded 3D Printing," *Advanced Materials*, vol. 30, no. 15, pp. 1–8, 2018, DOI: http://dx.doi.org/10.1002/adma.201706383.

[46] D. M. Vogt, Y. L. Park, and R. J. Wood, "Design and characterization of a soft multi-axis force sensor using embedded microfluidic channels," *IEEE Sensors Journal*, vol. 13, no. 10, pp. 4056–4064, 2013, DOI: http://dx.doi.org/10.1109/JSEN.2013.2272320.

[47] J. Weichart, M. Ott, T. Burger, and C. Hierold, "Towards Artificial Robotic Skin: Highly Sensitive Flexible Tactile Sensing Arrays with 3D Sensing Capabilities," in *IEEE MEMS*. IEEE, 2022, pp. 67–70, DOI: http://dx.doi.org/10.1109/MEMS51670.2022.9699826.

[48] J. H. Lau, *Fan-Out Wafer-Level Packaging*. Springer, 2018, DOI: http://dx.doi.org/10.1007/978-981-10-8884-1.

[49] H. Hedler, T. Meyer, and B. Vasquez, "Transfer wafer level packaging, US Patent 6,727,576," 2004.

[50] J.-c. Lin, J.-P. Hung, N.-W. Liu, Y.-C. Mao, W.-T. Shih, and T.-H. Tung, "Packaged semiconductor device with a molding compound and a method of forming the same, U.S. Patent 9,000,584," 2015.

[51] T. Braun, S. Raatz, S. Voges, R. Kahle, V. Bader, J. Bauer, K. F. Becker, T. Thomas, R. Aschenbrenner, and K. D. Lang, "Large area compression molding for Fan-out Panel Level Packing," *Proceedings - Electronic Components and Technology Conference*, vol. 2015-July, pp. 1077–1083, 2015, DOI: http://dx.doi.org/10.1109/ECTC.2015.7159728.

[52] J. Kim, I. Choi, J. Park, J. E. Lee, T. Jeong, J. Byun, Y. Ko, K. Hur, D. W. Kim, and K. S. Oh, "Fan-Out Panel Level Package with Fine Pitch Pattern," *Proceedings - Electronic Components and Technology Conference*, vol. 2018-May, pp. 52–57, 2018, DOI: http://dx.doi.org/10.1109/ECTC.2018.00016.

[53] J. Weichart, J. Weichart, A. Erhart, and K. Viehweger, "Preconditioning technologies for sputtered seed layers in FOPLP," *Proceedings - Electronic Components and Technology Conference*, vol. 2019-May, pp. 1833–1841, 2019, DOI: http://dx.doi.org/10.1109/ECTC.2019.00282.

[54] H. Burkard, W. Kapischke, and J. Link, "Large panel, highly flexible multilayer thin film boards," *2009 European Microelectronics and Packaging Conference, EMPC 2009*, 2009.

[55] N. Palavesam, S. Marin, D. Hemmetzberger, C. Landesberger, K. Bock, and C. Kutter, "Roll-to-roll processing of film substrates for hybrid integrated flexible electronics," *Flexible and Printed Electronics*, vol. 3, no. 1, 2018, DOI: http://dx.doi.org/10.1088/2058-8585/aaaa04.

[56] T. Braun, K.-f. Becker, O. Hoelck, S. Voges, R. Kahle, P. Graap, R. Aschenbrenner, T. Braun, M. Dreissigacker, and K.-d. Lang, "Fan-out Wafer Level Packaging - A Platform for Advanced Sensor Packaging," in *2019 IEEE 69th Electronic Components and Technology Conference (ECTC)*, 2019, pp. 861–867, DOI: http://dx.doi.org/10.1109/ECTC.2019.00135.

[57] A. Cardoso, S. Kroehnert, R. Pinto, E. Fernandes, and I. Barros, "Integration of MEMS/Sensors in Fan-Out wafer-level packaging technology based system-in-package (WLSiP)," *Proceedings of the 2016 IEEE 18th Electronics Packaging Technology Conference, EPTC 2016*, no. Figure 2, pp. 801–807, 2017, DOI: http://dx.doi.org/10.1109/EPTC.2016.7861591.

[58] R. J. Vetter, J. C. Williams, D. R. Kipke, P. J. Rousche, D. S. Pellinen, and D. P. Pivin, "Flexible polyimide-based intracortical electrode arrays with bioactive capability," *IEEE Transactions on Biomedical Engineering*, vol. 48, no. 3, pp. 361–371, 2001, DOI: http://dx.doi.org/10.1109/10.914800.

[59] B. Rubehn, C. Bosman, R. Oostenveld, P. Fries, and T. Stieglitz, "A MEMS-based flexible multichannel ECoG-electrode array," *Journal of Neural Engineering*, vol. 6, no. 3, 2009, DOI: http://dx.doi.org/10.1088/1741-2560/6/3/036003.

[60] X. Wang, A. W. Hirschberg, H. Xu, Z. Slingsby-Smith, A. Lecomte, K. Scholten, D. Song, and E. Meng, "A Parylene Neural Probe Array for Multi-Region Deep Brain Recordings," *Journal of Microelectromechanical Systems*, vol. 29, no. 4, pp. 499–513, 2020, DOI: http://dx.doi.org/10.1109/JMEMS.2020.3000235.

[61] D. A. Soscia, D. Lam, A. C. Tooker, H. A. Enright, M. Triplett, P. Karande, S. K. Peters, A. P. Sales, E. K. Wheeler, and N. O. Fischer, "A flexible 3-dimensional microelectrode array for: In vitro brain models," *Lab on a Chip*, vol. 20, no. 5, pp. 901–911, 2020, DOI: http://dx.doi.org/10.1039/c9lc01148j.

[62] P. Zhang, Y. Y. Lau, and R. M. Gilgenbach, "Analysis of current crowding in thin film contacts from exact field solution," *Journal of Physics D: Applied Physics*, vol. 48, no. 47, 2015, DOI: http://dx.doi.org/10.1088/0022-3727/48/47/475501.

[63] V. Manichelvan, "Analysis of the cost drivers in flexible electronics," Bachelor Thesis, ETH Zurich, 2022.

[64] R. Hopf, L. Bernardi, J. Menze, M. Zu, E. Mazza, and A. E. Ehret, "Experimental and theoretical analyses of the age-dependent large-strain behavior of Sylgard 184 (10 : 1) silicone elastomer," *Journal of mechanical behavior of biomedical materials*, vol. 60, pp. 425–437, 2016, DOI: http://dx.doi.org/10.1016/j.jmbbm.2016.02.022.

[65] L. Bernardi, R. Hopf, D. Sibilio, A. Ferrari, A. E. Ehret, and E. Mazza, "On the cyclic deformation behavior, fracture properties and cytotoxicity of silicone-based elastomers for biomedical applications," *Polymer Testing*, vol. 60, pp. 117–123, 2017, DOI: http://dx.doi.org/10.1016/j.polymertesting.2017.03.018.

[66] F. B. Coulter, B. S. Coulter, J. R. Marks, and A. Ianakiev, "Production Techniques for 3D Printed Inflatable Elastomer Structures: Part I-Fabricating Air-Permeable Forms and Coating with Inflatable Silicone Membranes via Spray Deposition," *3D Printing and Additive Manufacturing*, vol. 5, no. 1, pp. 5–15, 2018, DOI: http://dx.doi.org/10.1089/3dp.2017.0068.

[67] K. Choonee, R. R. Syms, M. M. Ahmad, and H. Zou, "Post processing of microstructures by PDMS spray deposition," *Sensors and Actuators, A: Physical*, vol. 155, no. 2, pp. 253–262, 2009, DOI: http://dx.doi.org/10.1016/j.sna.2009.08.029.

[68] O. A. Araromi, A. T. Conn, C. S. Ling, J. M. Rossiter, R. Vaidyanathan, and S. C. Burgess, "Spray deposited multilayered dielectric elastomer actuators," *Sensors and Actuators, A: Physical*, vol. 167, no. 2, pp. 459–467, 2011, DOI: http://dx.doi.org/10.1016/j.sna.2011.03.004.

[69] D. Wojcikiewicz, "Tactile feature extraction," Master Thesis, ETH Zurich, 2022.

[70] L. Kehrbein, "Development of a characterization setup and testing of arti cial robotic skin," Master thesis, ETH Zurich, 2020.

[71] M. Hueppin, "Analysis of the vibration sensing capability of tactile sensors," Bachelor Thesis, ETH Zurich, 2021.

[72] Agilent Technologies, *Impedance Measurement Handbook - A guide to measurement technology and techniques, 4th edition*, 2009.

[73] P. Sivananthaguru, "Electrical Readout of Tactile Sensor Networks," Master Thesis, ETH Zurich, 2021.

[74] T. Schilcher, "RF applications in digital signal processing," *CAS 2007 - CERN Accelerator School: Digital Signal Processing, Proceedings*, pp. 249–283, 2008.

[75] R. S. Dahiya and M. Valle, *Robotic Tactile Sensing.* Springer, 2013, DOI: http://dx.doi.org/10.1007/978-94-007-0579-1.

[76] Z. Su, J. A. Fishel, T. Yamamoto, and G. E. Loeb, "Use of tactile feedback to control exploratory movements to characterize object compliance," *Frontiers in Neurorobotics*, vol. 6, no. JULY, pp. 1–9, 2012, DOI: http://dx.doi.org/10.3389/fnbot.2012.00007.

Publications & Contributions

Peer-reviewed journal publications

1. Weichart J, Roman C, Hierold C. Tactile Sensing With Scalable Capacitive Sensor Arrays on Flexible Substrates. J Microelectromechanical Syst. 2021

2. Weichart J, Sivananthaguru P, Coulter FB, Burger T, Hierold C. Artificial fingertip with high resolution tactile sensing capabilities. **Submitted to Soft Robot. Nov. 2022**;

Refereed conference proceedings

1. Weichart J, Ott M, Burger T, Hierold C. Towards Artificial Robotic Skin: Highly Sensitive Flexible Tactile Sensing Arrays with 3D Sensing Capabilities. IEEE MEMS 2022

Conference Talks

1. Weichart J, Ott M, Burger T, Hierold C. Towards Artificial Robotic Skin: Highly Sensitive Flexible Tactile Sensing Arrays with 3D Sensing Capabilities. IEEE MEMS 2022

2. Weichart J. Development of a sensitive artificial fingertip . MaP Symposium 2021

Patents

1. Sensor System for a Three-Dimensional Device. Patent No. EP/2021/166297. Nominated for Top 5 Patents of ETH Zurich at Spark Award 2022.

Accepted Proposals

1. TACTFUL: Advancing robotic manipulation with spatial and temporal rich tactile sensing. ETH Zurich Collaborative Grant, Sept. 2022. 633.4 kCHF

Student projects supervised

1. Gustav Pacher-Theinburg: Overview of Characterization Setups for Tactile Sensors, October 2019

2. Severin Siegrist: Simulation environment for a tactile sensing cell in soft material, December 2019

3. Bruna Azevedo: Design of a characterization setup for artificial robotic skin, April 2020

4. Cyrille Grumbach: Fabrication of Polymer Sacrificial Layers for Artificial Robotic Skin, July 2020

5. Marcel Ott: Impedance Measurement System for Low Capacitance Tactile Sensor Arrays, June 2020

6. Leo Fent: Overview on Tactile Sensors for Artificial Skin Applications, December 2020

7. Ayeshabanu Walikar: Fabrication and optimization of an interconnection substrate, Jan 2021

8. Lorenz Kehrbein: Development of a characterization setup and testing of artificial robotic skin, April 2021

9. Tim Groenveld: Spray Head Design for a Silicone Spray Coating System, April 2021

10. Dominik Wojcikiewicz: Software interface for a spray coater, June 2021

11. David Zürcher: Design, simulation and fabrication of an artificial finger, August 2021

12. Pragash Sivananthaguru: Electrical Readout of Tactile Sensor Networks, November 2021

13. Tim Groenveld: Development and Characterization of a Silicone Spray Coating Process, July 2021

14. Matthias Hüppin: Analysis of the vibration sensing capability of tactile sensors, December 2021

15. Vibuja Manichelvan: Analysis of the cost drivers in flexible electronics, June 2022

16. Felix Mähr: Influence of skin layers on static and dynamic characteristics of artificial robotic skin, June 2022

17. Curdin Cavelti: Development of a real-time plotting environment for artificial robotic skin, June 2022

18. Andri Caviezel: Simulation and Fabrication of an Artificial Finger with Integrated Tactile Sensors, June 2022

19. Louis Colbach: Capacitive Array to Digital Conversion System for Electronic Skin, Sept 2022

20. Dominik Wojcikiewicz: Tactile feature extraction, November 2022

21. Yi Lin Cao: Study on the Integration of Temperature Sensing in Artificial Robotic Skin, December 2022

22. Leon Niebergall: Design of an injection moldable artificial finger, June 2023 (exp.)

23. Moritz Junker: Design and implementation of a 5-axis characterization setup for machine learning on artificial robotic fingers, Sept 2023 (exp.)

Curriculum Vitae

Personal Details

Name	Johannes Weichart
Birth	12.01.1991, Hamburg, Germany
Citizenship	Liechtenstein
Marital Status	unmarried

Education

03/2019 – 05/2023	**Micro and Nanosystems, ETH Zurich, Switzerland** PhD Dissertation "Artificial Fingertip with Embedded High Resolution Tactile Sensing"
09/2013 – 09/2015	**MSc Mechanical Engineering, ETH Zurich, Switzerland** Focus: Mechatronics & Production technology
09/2014 – 12/2014	**Exchange Semester, University of Toronto, Canada**
09/2009 – 06/2012	**BSc Mechanical Engineering, ETH Zurich, Switzerland** Focus: Focus Project "Skye" and robotics

Work Experience

03/2019 – 05/2023	**Micro and Nanosystems, ETH Zurich, Switzerland** Research and teaching assistant
02/2019 – 03/2021	**Evatec AG, Trübbach, Switzerland** Plasma technology consultant
02/2016 – 01/2019	**Evatec AG, Trübbach, Switzerland** Process engineer Strategic Projects

02/2013 – 08/2013	**Buehler AG, Uzwil , Switzerland**
	Internship Corporate Technology, development of novel food processing machine
09/2012 – 01/2013	**Project realize 'Skye', Shanghai, China**
	Drone controls and simulation environment development
08/2012 – 09/2012	**Hilti AG, Schaan, Liechtenstein**
	Internship Advanced Mechatronics

Languages

German	Native Language
English	Business Proficiency
French	Intermediate
Spanish	Basic

Scientific Reports on Micro and Nanosystems

edited by Prof. Dr. Christofer Hierold
ETH Zürich
Micro and Nanosystems

Vol. 26:   Silke Christina Wouters, **New Type of Three-Axis Hall Sensor Designed for High-Accuracy Magnetic Field Measurements.** 1st Edition 2017. XXII, 162 pages. € 64,00. ISBN 978-3-86628-593-4

Vol. 27:   Moritz Thielen, **Thermal and Electrical Energy Converters and Interfaces for the Internet of Humans.** 1st Edition 2018. XVI, 208 pages. € 64,00. ISBN 978-3-86628-612-2

Vol. 28:   Verena Maiwald, **A Microelectromechanical Switch for Bandpass Vibration Detection.** 1st Edition 2018. XVI, 164 pages. € 64,00. ISBN 978-3-86628-614-6

Vol. 29:   Michelle Müller, **Micromechanical broadband vibration amplitude-amplifier for microseismic and acoustic emission detection.** 1st Edition 2019. XVIII, 168 pages. € 64,00. ISBN 978-3-86628-627-6

Vol. 30:   Silvan Marc Staufert, **Conformal Parylene-C Media Separating Membranes for Pressure Sensing Applications in Ventricular Assist Devices.** 1st Edition 2019. XVIII, 150 pages. € 64,00. ISBN 978-3-86628-636-8

Vol. 31:   Lalit Kumar**, Energy Dissipation, Clamping and Motional Currents in Suspended Room Temperature Carbon Nanotube Resonators.** 1st Edition 2019. XXIV, 182 pages. € 64,00. ISBN 978-3-86628-650-4

Vol. 32:   Sebastian Eberle, **Ultra-clean suspended carbon nanotube gas sensors - concept for large scale fabrication and sensor characterization.** 1st Edition 2019. XX, 180 pages. € 64,00. ISBN 978-3-86628-659-7

Vol. 33:   Laura Vera Jenni, **Optimization of CNT Contacts in Suspended CNTFETs and Post Dry-Transfer Processing**. 1st Edition 2019. XXII, 170 pages. € 64,00. ISBN 978-3-86628-660-3

Vol. 34:   Ian Aleksander Mihailovic, **Ag/BiSe memristors for sensor data storage: a novel concept for zero-power sense-log devices.** 1st Edition 2022. XX, 146 pages. € 64,00. ISBN 978-3-86628-769-3

Vol. 35:   Stefan Nedelcu, **Energy efficient analog mixed-signal front ends for CNT-FET NO2 air-quality nanosensors.** 1st Edition 2022. XXVIII, 236 pages. € 64,00. ISBN 978-3-86628-779-2

http://www.hartung-gorre.de
Hartung-Gorre Verlag, Konstanz